Crosscurrents / MODERN CRITIQUES

Harry T. Moore, *General Editor*

RICHARD ALDINGTON
Selected Critical Writings,
1928–1960

EDITED BY

Alister Kershaw

WITH A PREFACE BY
Harry T. Moore

SOUTHERN ILLINOIS UNIVERSITY PRESS
Carbondale and Edwardsville

FEFFER & SIMONS, INC.
London and Amsterdam

For permission to reprint copyright material, acknowledgments
are due to the following: The estate of the late Glenn Hughes
("Remy de Gourmont"); Times Newspapers Ltd., London
("Aldous Huxley" and "Wyndham Lewis"); Doubleday & Co.,
Inc. ("Somerset Maugham"); The Viking Press, Inc. ("Oscar
Wilde"); The Meredith Press ("Walter Pater"); Editions
Seghers, Paris ("D. H. Lawrence"); Two Cities, Paris ("Law-
rence Durrell").

Contents

Preface

Toward the end of his life, the poet Richard Aldington (1892–1962) became one of the most controversial authors in many a year. His first novel, Death of a Hero, had won international attention in 1929 as an important satiric statement against war, and was generally accepted on its merits. But in the 1950s Aldington became the subject of frequent and violent condemnation.

This began with his biography of D. H. Lawrence in 1950, which irritated a good many people, for reasons I could never understand. (I gave it what I considered a favorable write-up in the Saturday Review, though Aldington didn't like it.) His troubles continued with his double biography of Norman Douglas and "Pino" Orioli, which Aldington rather unfortunately called Pinorman. This ruefully humorous portrait of Douglas whooped up the anger of his supporters.

This antagonism is also strong against the man who wrote the book whose full title is Lawrence of Arabia: A Biographical Inquiry (amusingly enough, this came out as Lawrence l'imposteur in the French edition). Because of the rage against this book, denigrating a "national hero," there is great rage against Richard Aldington and all he wrote. Why?

Partly because of a conspiracy. Aldington wasn't paranoid in imagining such a thing existed; indeed, he was not just imagining. For the Lawrence clique—what he called the Lawrence Bureau—had even attempted to stop publication of the book. Alister Kershaw refers to this effort toward the end of his Introduction that follows; he mentions Robert Graves and the late B. H. Liddell Hart. But there were others. The full story was to have been told in the recently published book by Phillip Knightley and Colin Simpson, The Secret

Lives of Lawrence of Arabia, but what was originally their twentieth chapter, a detailed account that named names, was withdrawn from their volume because, according to the authors' lawyers, it's quite all right under English law to wage surreptitious war against an author, but all wrong to reveal that this took place!

I have the "suppressed chapter" at hand; it is a most disturbing document, for it shows how Liddell Hart and others tried to influence the publishing house of Collins not to bring out the book. But William Collins, a rather tough old man, refused to be intimidated, and published it. Then the infuriated reviews began, as planned.

This is to me the most appalling part of the whole story. Perhaps one doesn't have to be so totally detached, these days, as James Gibbons Huneker, who refused to dine at Richard Mansfield's Riverside Drive residence (the location dates the anecdote) because he would later have to write reviews of Mansfield's stage performances!

There should, however, be some circumspection. What happened in the case of Aldington's biography of Lawrence of Arabia?

There is, among others, the case of B. H. Liddell Hart, a previous Lawrence biographer and one of Lawrence's good friends. Hart, who had tried to block publication of Aldington's book, had the gall to "review" it in the London Magazine, and then he extended his attack, transoceanically, to repeat his criticism in the Atlantic. But his reviews at least remained what Schopenhauer in "The Art of Controversy" called ad rem, concerned with the subject, rather than ad hominem, attacking the man. Still, it was ungraceful for someone who had tried to stifle the book to turn up later as its reviewer. Robert Graves, who had suggested calling in lawyers to stop British publication of the volume, also "reviewed" it in England and America. In the latter country it was surprising to find so ordinarily circumspect a journal as the New Republic printing such ad hominem vituperation as Graves's characterization of the book as "the self-portrait of a bitter, bedridden, leering, asthmatic, elderly hang-man-of-letters—the live dog who thinks himself better than the dead lion because he can at least scratch himself and snarl." In our time, "criticism" has rarely gone to such a vicious extreme; and, to those of us who knew Richard Aldington, so unwarranted and inaccurate an extreme.

Touching the personal note for a moment again, what was Aldington's motive in writing this biography? The whole idea came from Alister Kershaw's suggestion that Aldington write such a book, as Aldington makes plain in his "Introductory Letter to Alister Kershaw." Aldington had at first hesitated, for reasons he explains in that letter, but at last Kershaw persuaded him to undertake the task. The important thing to remember is that he began with no bias against his subject, as Kershaw explains in the Introduction to the present book.

Aldington's conclusions about Lawrence are expressed mildly enough in its pages, but the emotional frenzy of Lawrence's supporters made it seem that Aldington had not presented his discoveries in a coolly reasonable way.

I had some experience with the enduring anti-Aldington ferocity while in London in 1966, years later. On Sunday July 10, the Observer carried a review by its foreign editor, one Robert Stephens. He was discussing an anti-Lawrence book by an Arab, Suleiman Mousa, published by Oxford University Press. One of Suleiman Mousa's main points is the same as one of Aldington's, that Lawrence was a fraud. Robert Stephens didn't agree with much of Mousa's findings, but he was fairly polite about that, though he was not so to Aldington, who he said had written "with unconvincing venom" in his own "notorious book." Further, "Aldington's diatribe exposed a deep private pool of vitriol." Although I knew that all attempts to defend Aldington's carefully dispassionate study of Lawrence had been smothered by the British press for more than a decade, I wrote a very short letter to the Observer, which it certainly had space to print. I asked merely that Robert Stephens provide page references in Aldington's book indicating which passages contained any examples of "venom" and "vitriol." My letter was not printed, for the obvious reason that Stephens could provide no such references.

This is only one of the many examples of the attempts to

muffle any possible defense of Aldington, and one of the reasons that I, like Alister Kershaw, am spending so much time in trying to show, before we consider Richard Aldington as a literary critic, that he wasn't the villain his enemies have made him appear to be.

Amusingly enough, one of my attempts to defend him backfired. In a long reminiscence which first appeared in the Texas Quarterly and was later included in Alister Kershaw's Southern Illinois University Press book, Richard Aldington: An Intimate Portrait, I wrote in 1962 or 1963:

His recent books on Norman Douglas and on Lawrence of Arabia had been harshly attacked in the British press, and he had been called an embittered and frustrated man. But the Richard Aldington I met on that August day of 1958 at Cosne [Nièvre] and on several later visits there in the next few years, and with whom I was to exchange many letters in that period, was not at all frustrated and embittered. Certainly he was critical of some phases of civilization, a mark of intelligence and sensitivity, but he expressed himself without dogmatic frenzy, and he showed no corroding grievance. His wit was sharp, his tone cheerful.

I don't think there is anything in what I said which is in the least ambiguous.

But, shortly after the memoir appeared, I wrote to an old friend of Aldington's and mine, asking whether I might copy some of his letters from Aldington, since I was preparing both a biography of him and an edition of his lively letters—and the friend wrote back angrily criticizing me for saying that "Richard was bitter." Now, I ask you—as the phrase goes— did I in any way hint that Richard Aldington was "bitter"? On the contrary, as my text shows. But perhaps more people should take lessons in reading.

Richard Aldington's literary essays might well serve as a model text for such lessons. It might be said from the first that he was for the most part an expository critic, leading us along various literary paths and pointing out interesting and important sights on the way. Further, he sometimes makes rewarding discoveries.

Remy de Gourmont, the subject of the first essay in this book, was an enthusiasm of Aldington's, who translated his work into English (as did Ezra Pound and Aldous Huxley). Gourmont, virtually a recluse because of his affliction of lupus, never met his ardent young English admirer. In 1929, fourteen years after Gourmont's death, Aldington brought out a two-volume edition (now unfortunately out of print) of his translations of Gourmont's work. The reputation of Remy de Gourmont, whom T. S. Eliot once called "the critical consciousness of a generation," is still a good one, as attested by Glenn S. Burne's useful study of him in the Crosscurrents series. In the present volume, Aldington's essay is a valuable introduction to this writer.

The piece on Aldous Huxley is rather slight, actually a review of one of his earlier volumes of essays, with a sly poke at Aldington's former friend T. S. Eliot, whose name is not mentioned. The next section is an interesting discussion of Wyndham Lewis' The Apes of God, a roman à clef which raised a furor. The discussion is in two parts, the first a review and the second a discussion or continuation of the review, which Lewis had indicated, in an interview, that Aldington had misunderstood; but Aldington was really on his side. He ends with a note of hope for Lewis' future, which was not so great a one as expected, although he lived on to write at least one more interesting novel, Self Condemned (1954). Today we have to strain Lewis' work through a colander of realization that in the late 1930s he was an eager supporter of Hitler, which is hard to forgive in a man who had reached maturity by that time; for by then Hitler could be seen for what he was, and the later opening up of the corpse camps only helped to give a final effluvium to his reputation.

The Somerset Maugham essay is a tribute to the popular novelist, written as a pamphlet for Maugham's American publishers, then Doubleday, Doran and Company. The fact that this was company-written doesn't mean that Richard Aldington had to stuff it with things he didn't mean; he was always a fervent admirer of Maugham, and this is only one of several pieces he wrote about him. Myself, I've never thought highly of Maugham's work and used to argue about it with Richard Aldington. I have read and can read Maugham, however, and a recent review of a republication of some of his early stories, found me (in the Saturday Review) a little more tolerant of his work than I had been for many years. Pointing out that "leading critics have never granted [Maugham] much in the way of stature, even for the famous novel Of Human Bondage," the review went on to say that, today, "many of his frequently praised short stories seem to deserve no more than the word competent, which used to irritate Maugham when a reviewer applied it to them. Yet some of them are still entertainingly readable."

The long essay on Oscar Wilde is an extremely fascinating one, written not long after Aldington had turned to biography as one of his principal modes of expression. It is a good, clear, informative piece of writing, with various new perspectives, and written in Aldington's best and most animated manner.

Of the essay on Pater, I can say only that it is excellent. I don't know anything better on the subject, and doubt if such exists. The essay on Jane Austen is shorter, but still very useful because of its observations and rearrangements of perspective.

With Roy Campbell, Lawrence Durrell, and D. H. Lawrence, we are on somewhat different ground, for Aldington is here writing about people he knew whose writings he admired. But this doesn't keep him from saying many pertinent things about those men and their works.

My one-time reservations in regard to Campbell took life from his voluntary service in Franco's army during the Spanish Civil War of the 1930s. Again, it is difficult to overlook the case of a mature man, who should "know better," who chose a cause so obviously marked by viciousness. Admittedly, many of us who favored the Loyalist side—the properly elected Spanish government which had a constitution based on that of the United States—didn't know then how thoroughly the authoritarian Soviet influence would take over in the course of time. In my own case, it was some time later that I read George Orwell's Homage to Catalonia, first published in 1938, a year before the conflict ended—this book was a trenchant comment on Soviet intervention. It was 1940 before we had For Whom the Bell Tolls, in which poor old confused Ernest Hemingway, no longer a master of the clear, crisp prose of his earlier works, wrote about the Spanish war in occasionally compelling scenes, but mostly with repetitious befuddlement; but one thing that came out of all this was a realization of the part played by such Communist authoritarians as André Marty. It took a long time, however, for many of us to become disillusioned with Loyalist Spain. But, whatever conclusions may be drawn from this, there is no human excuse for a Roy Campbell to fight on the side of Franco's Falangists. How many poets or intellectuals from other countries did so? But let's say that Campbell somewhat cleared his record as a human being by later volunteering to fight for the British against Hitler.

Richard Aldington's essay on Roy Campbell is not so much criticism, even critical explication, as a genial remembrance of a friend killed in an automobile accident seven months earlier. It is pleasant to read, and it projects the geniality of Campbell's personality, and here and there it makes some helpful comments on his poetry.

The discussion of Lawrence Durrell, dating from a time when three of the books of his Alexandria tetralogy were completed, is a significant early recognition of the abilities of a younger man who can write of exotic places with the appropriate tints and cadences, and whose use of language is poetic and precise. This essay is a welcome addition to Durrell criticism.

To write comprehensively of the relationship of Aldington with D. H. Lawrence would take more space than that allotted here, which is already overstepping its boundaries. The piece which Alister Kershaw has chosen for inclusion in this volume is Aldington's 1960 Introduction (originally written in the French he could use so expertly) to F.-J. Temple's excellent book (written in French) about Lawrence. This is one of the last times Aldington wrote about his friend from Nottinghamshire with whom his relationship ended rather abruptly just a little more than a year before Lawrence died. Aldington had first written about him in 1927, three years before Lawrence's death, in a small book subtitled An Indiscretion ("It's more about you, my dear Richard, than about me," Lawrence wrote). Aldington dealt with Lawrence at some length in his own autobiography, Life For Life's Sake, a luminously witty volume first published in 1941. Then, in 1950, he wrote his Portrait of a Genius, But . . . This was a full-length biography of Lawrence, a bright and living book, but unfortunately containing no newly researched material. Yet it was a vital book, for despite his frequent detachment in literary matters, Richard Aldington could often be involved in what he was writing about, and could be genially warm. But he was always informative and essentially critical.

Alister Kershaw has given us a fine presentation of him in this volume. But now let's let Alister say some more about him and his work.

HARRY T. MOORE

Southern Illinois University
April 26, 1970

Introduction

If the expression had not somehow become frowzy and a bit absurd, Richard Aldington might be described as preeminently a "man of letters"—the last, perhaps, who will trouble the jubilant illiteracy of this age of "blind mouths." The term would seem to be appropriate to Aldington partly because of his lifelong devotion to literature, a devotion which was simultaneously generous and discriminating, and partly because of his own formidable achievements in an exceptionally wide range of genres. His work, indeed, is so many-sided that, inevitably, most people are familiar with only one or two aspects of it and it may be worthwhile therefore to provide an outline of his career.

Like most writers, Aldington began as a poet, his earliest work appearing (on the recommendation of Ezra Pound) in the Chicago magazine, *Poetry*, in 1912 when he was nineteen; unlike most writers, he remained a poet, although he destroyed the poems written in the last years of his life and no copies, as far as I know, exist. His poems are largely ignored these days by the anthologists, always so comically timid and conventional in rejecting all work that hasn't been officially stamped and countersigned by the literary bureaucrats, and he rarely figures in the academics' piffling little "surveys" and "notes on"—but intellectuals, most of them, are eternal simpletons who can be brainwashed and bamboozled into admiring or deploring anything. Not that it matters. The poetry of Aldington's contemporaries is examined, studied, annotated, and interpreted; among those whose tastes are spontaneous and undictated, Aldington's poetry is *read*.

Shortly after his early poems were published, Aldington produced the first of his scholarly—and, once again, supremely readable—translations. These eventually came to include works drawn from modern and medieval French, Provençal, Italian, Latin, and Greek, prefaced very often by no less scholarly and readable introductions which (as Lawrence Durrell has recorded) provided a good many people with passports to worlds which might otherwise well have remained inaccessible to them.

In 1929 appeared *Death of a Hero*, a work as revolutionary in its way as Céline's *Voyage au bout de la nuit* and infused with a similar desolate rage—clear evidence, according to D. H. Lawrence, that Aldington was heading for a lunatic asylum although Wyndham Lewis, Arnold Bennett, H. G. Wells and others were too obtuse to see it as anything but a major novel "impossible to ignore."

It was followed by other novels—*The Colonel's Daughter*, *All Men are Enemies*, *Women Must Work* and *Very Heaven* among them—which somehow manage to combine what must, I suppose, be called "social criticism" with an intense personal fervor and a Lawrentian insight into the vital relations of individuals, and by two volumes of short stories—the bleak *Roads to Glory* and the lethally satiric *Soft Answers*.

From 1943, when his life of the Duke of Wellington was published, Aldington devoted himself almost entirely to a series of biographies, although a number of distinguished anthologies, brilliantly introduced, were also forthcoming during the same period. Up to a certain stage, the biographies were what is known as "well received" (the *Wellington* was awarded the James Tait Black prize and an *Introduction to Mistral*, the Prix de Gratitude Mistralienne) although various people were always gratifyingly outraged by Aldington's inability to turn out bland obsequious panegyrics. In 1955, however, *Lawrence of Arabia* was published and it will be necessary to discuss this at some length later on.

Throughout his career, Aldington was simultaneously producing a considerable body of critical writing from which a

very small selection has been assembled in the present volume. It is pitifully straightforward and unpretentious stuff
when compared to the alembicated commentaries which set
contemporary innocents ooh-ing and ah-ing in simpleminded
wonder: there isn't enough obscurity and confusion in it on
which to found a single parasitic "school" of criticism. But
Aldington took the modest view that the function of the
critic was to direct attention toward what he considered to
be valuable work, to indicate why he considered it valuable,
and then, having provided potential readers with an opportunity to share in a new experience, to step out of the picture. His successors, of course, hold that the only purpose of
original work is to furnish a platform on which the critic can
caper about and do his little "turn."

Such pouter-pigeon performances obviously call for a mini-
mum of knowledge and taste—just enough, in fact, to enable
the critic to work in an allusion to whatever literary pop star
has been momentarily taken up by the trend-setters. Anything beyond that is undemocratic and reactionary, if not
downright fascistic: when Aldington's memoirs were published recently in England, one reviewer was altogether unable to repress his sturdy proletarian indignation over the fact
that the author had quoted a line by *Dante* . . .

The ugly truth is that Aldington was so deplorably out of
tune with the age that he didn't even know it was wrong to
quote Dante. He had read prodigiously in half-a-dozen languages, and had compounded the offense by doing so out of
an entirely unofficial passion for literature. As if this were not
bad enough, he carried insolence to the point of believing
that literature should be judged in terms of literature: for
him, a bad book didn't become good simply because it was
written by a Negro, a Cuban revolutionary, or some raucous
representative of "youth." Conversely, he rejected the notion
that a good book becomes bad if it should turn out that the
author has never thrown a brick or carried a banner. (Asked
by an uneasy interviewer if there was any danger of a right-
wing genius jumping out of the dark and frightening respectable people to death, the preposterous Sartre, who can always
be relied on to trip over his own fatuous dialect, gave his

personal assurance not long ago that the Marxist tribal ju-ju would never allow anyone deviating from left-wing conformism to have the slightest trace of talent.)

Finally, in discussing other writers, Aldington gave them, rather than himself, the center of the stage. Obviously, his own tastes, his own judgments, reveal themselves; but he never indulged—was never tempted to indulge—in the flip, *m'as-tu-vu* circus acts of the intellectual Gugusses who are running things these days. When Aldington wrote about Roy Campbell, say, it was not in order to acquaint the reader with his own views on vegetarianism, birth control or nuclear warfare, but in order to communicate his enthusiasm for *Campbell*.

The fact, incidentally, that Campbell was execrated by the sub-literati naturally didn't worry Aldington in the least; but it was equally characteristic of him that he could as readily recognize the merits of a writer as deplorably successful as Somerset Maugham. Much it mattered to him to find himself in conflict with the cliques—or in agreement with the public.

This independence of judgment is accompanied in Aldington's critical writing by an altogether admirable capacity for generous appreciation. He never puffs or propagandizes, he simply succeeds in transmitting his own enthusiasm and thereby awakening in the reader a desire to participate in that intensely felt pleasure. As a general rule, he simply didn't bother to discuss those writers whom he found boring or exasperating or meretricious since he saw no point in producing dessicated essays on how *not* to enjoy.

It is particularly grotesque, therefore, that he should now be habitually represented, at any rate in the British press, as a surly denigrator. The explanation lies in the circumstances surrounding his biography of *Lawrence of Arabia* to which I have already referred.

Aldington began writing this book, as he explains in the introduction and as I can myself confirm, with no prejudice against Lawrence; but, as his investigations proceeded, he was led to conclude that the man was a compulsive liar and that his reputation was fraudulent.

In publishing the "biographical inquiry" which put forward this view (one which has never been successfully refuted) he was guilty, however, of something worse than insufficient reverence for a "national hero"; his real offense was to have simultaneously exposed the stupefying credulity of all those who had been taken in by Lawrence's self-glorification and who had incautiously recorded their besotted admiration.

In the introduction to a new edition of his own pious work on Lawrence, Lowell Thomas artlessly furnishes a glimpse of the hysterical consultations which took place among these discomfited gulls; but he is not sufficiently ingenuous to mention the efforts made to bully Aldington's publisher into abandoning the book, the blustering vows to exercise physical reprisals, the solemn consideration given to the possibility of a Royal Commission being appointed. Still less does he allude to a grimy little arrangement whereby, at the behest of Liddell Hart, Robert Graves, and other influential hero-worshippers, reviewers pledged themselves *in advance* to attack Aldington's biography—their servile acquiescence being duly recognized by the award of a picture of Lawrence's camel or some such ludicrous fetish.

Since there was no hope of rebutting Aldington, it was decided that the most effective technique for discrediting him would be to assert, over and over again, that he was, had always been, an incorrigible curmudgeon, a rancorous belittler of great men, so that the Lawrence book would be seen as merely another bit of spite which nobody need take seriously. True, he had been one of the first to salute the genius of Marcel Proust, had consistently defended the other Lawrence (the bad one), had written with the utmost respect of Voltaire, of Remy de Gourmont—not to mention the classic authors discussed in his *Literary Studies and Reviews* and *French Studies and Reviews*—but it was rightly felt that not many people in a God-fearing country would be familiar with these writings compared to the millions who daily spell out the irrefutable truths of the British press.

In the long run, Aldington's book demolished the myth of Lawrence once and for all and nobody now attempts to deny that the latter was a monument of mendacity (indeed, Malcolm Muggeridge recently reproached Aldington for believing too much!) but the myth of Aldington's "bitterness" and "spitefulness" persists. In the present volume, those who, out of malice or ignorance, have helped to perpetuate it have their answer.

The editor and publishers wish to express their gratitude to David Arkell, Esq. for his invaluable assistance in preparing this book.

Paris, France
October 1969

ALISTER KERSHAW

Richard Aldington

Selected Critical Writings

1928–1960

1

Remy de Gourmont

The author I am to discuss has no biography. He will never be a subject for the novelist-critics who study an author's works only to imagine his life instead of examining his life in order to understand his works. Remy de Gourmont was not what is called "a great figure." His life can almost be told in a sentence: "He was born, he grew up, he read, he observed, he thought, he wrote and he died." He was genuinely indifferent to those gratifications of vanity known as "honors." In the capital of the vainest nation of Europe he lived the life of a philosophical hermit, thereby proving that it is sometimes possible to avoid the notoriety and social engagements which other writers find so unpleasantly inevitable. Yet he was not a mere bookworm. He was an interested spectator and a critic of men and women. Perhaps he saw many curious and neglected aspects of the game of life because he was a spectator and not a player. His incapacity for action was as immense as his capacity for reflection. He was not one of the many fortunate people who can act without thinking. He found it necessary to think long before he acted and the more he thought the less it seemed necessary to act at all. The only occupation—besides his lifelong occupation of authorship—he ever indulged in was that of assistant librarian at the Bibliothèque Nationale. I believe the regulations were so mild that this "occupation" only meant that he read and wrote at the public library what he could otherwise have read and written in his own library. And he early contrived to lose even this gentle occupation by publishing an article which his superiors thought sufficiently unpatriotic to warrant his dismissal from an official post.

Pamphlet published under the title *Remy de Gourmont: A Modern Man of Letters* (Seattle: University of Washington Book Store, 1928).

If we may judge from Gourmont's books he must more than once have been seriously attracted by persons of the opposite sex. Yet he never married and he formed few of those lighter alliances which occupy so much space in most biographies of authors. Here again thought deflected action. He was much more interested in analyzing his emotions than in the emotions themselves. If Mr. Weller, senior, had possessed half Gourmont's passion for self-analysis he would have been secure from the most designing widows. Falling in love is one of the mainsprings of human action, as all long-established governments realize. In the words of Thomas Love Peacock, "the safety of the State depends upon the preservation of female chastity." When Gourmont fell in love his incapacity for action and his delight in analyzing himself into immobility asserted themselves. I seem to behold him in my mind's eye, returning hastily and in alarm to his book-ramparted fortress in the rue des Saints-Pères to arm himself fourfold against this dangerous seduction to embrace a life of action. His defense was peculiar to himself. Sometimes he would defend himself by composing an erotic novel where the characters are embodied ideas, where everything is discussed and nothing happens. Sometimes, if hard pressed, he wrote queer, quasi-philosophic love letters, so remote from the soft charms of domesticity that they would repel the most predatory female. Beaten, apparently, to his last line of trenches, on one occasion he composed a highly technical biological treatise which he called *Physique de l'Amour*. He ought to have called it "A Physic for Love"; for I have never read anything more likely to chill the passion of the most ardent lover.

By these curious and complicated devices Gourmont avoided taking that step which inevitably condemns a man to a life of action in order to protect a woman and her children. I have made this explanation because, owing to the choice of translators and the depravity of man, Gourmont is chiefly known as an erotic novelist. This is the least interesting side of his very complex literary personality. I do not say that Gourmont's erotic books are devoid of interest, but they are not solely interesting because of their eroticism. Unadul-

terated eroticism in literature must inevitably become tedi-
ous to all but immature and vulgar minds. Gourmont's
novels cannot be ignored because they form a considerable
fraction of his work, but they are interesting, not only from
their eroticism, but from their subtlety of analysis, their
beauty of form and style, and above all from the multitude
of ideas, many of them original, which he expresses. These
works have obtained for Gourmont the reputation of being
the usual Parisian man-about-town. Nothing could be farther
from the truth. He was a sort of lay-monk, an untonsured
Benedictine vowed to the service of literature. His passion
was for ideas, his method critical and analytic. His theory of
the dissociation of ideas—his most valuable contribution to
thought—was a formulation of his delight in analysis. For
Gourmont, sex was an idea, a formidable, gigantic, dangerous and therefore infinitely attractive idea, which he "dissociated" indefatigably at the different stages of his evolution
as a philosopher.

I have used the word "philosopher" regretfully. Having
deprived Gourmont of the dubious laurel-wreath of Petro-
nius, I am not going to present him with the halo of Aristotle.
I am not going to claim that he is highly important as a
philosopher. If I am to make clear my view of Gourmont I
must insist upon his complexity, upon the variety of his
mind. He was both artist and philosopher, both poet and
critic. He has left poems, novels, literary criticism, dialogues,
essays in psychology and anthropology, ethics and biology; he
was a sceptic who dabbled happily in mysticism and theol-
ogy; a poet with an almost excessive respect for logic. We
cannot say that any one of these aspects of his complexity is
more marked than the others. He was more a poet in his
youth, more a philosopher in his maturity; but he wrote
poems in the last year of his life and some of his earliest
writing is critical. This plenitude and versatility of mind
make him so interesting. He was an encyclopaedic man of
letters, the Diderot of Symbolism. His mind was an exchange
and mart of ideas. He possessed erudition almost as remote
and useless as Robert Burton's; and he was nearly as self-cen-
tered as Montaigne. Yet, like all the best minds of his

generation, he strove with ardor and persistence to learn the best that had been thought and was being thought in Europe.

He has defined his own mind in a passage on that well-worn topic of Classic versus Romantic:

The classic or traditional Latin considers life as a series of alternating states, indifferent, happy, sad, comic, tragic or passionate. These states are balanced in him, efface one another, neutralize one another. He is always ready to pass from laughter to tears, from day-dreaming to meditation, from pleasure to business, from passion to gallantry. Everything balances in this fortunate nature, which is apt for all sensations and sentiments except one, boredom. "Boredom came to life one day from uniformity." Notice the prodigious variety of Voltaire's work, which goes from mathematics to mischief—he is a type of the Latin, the refined Latin, the Gallo-Roman.

The Romantic is the man who cannot vary either his sentiments or his ideas. He struggles always in the same direction, exhausts himself, becomes exasperated, bored, and falls into the pit of despair he has digged himself. He is the man with fixed ideas. Like the early Christian, the Romantic thinks only of himself and his eternal salvation, but he places eternity in his own lifetime and transposes duration into intensity. He tries to condense centuries into minutes and wears himself out in the part of a blind Danaïde. He pours floods of wine into a thimble, drinks and is amazed to find that he has scarcely moistened his tongue. What a type of the Romantic is Chateaubriand's René, who might have found so much amusement in life and yet was so much bored by it! When a man tries to live of himself, on himself, and for himself, he is always bored. There is no pleasure except in others; all pleasure is social.

The antithesis is more interesting as psychology than as literary criticism. Even in French literature, the only literature for which the "Classic-Romantic" controversy has any lasting importance, where will you find a more exasperated temperament and more fixed ideas than in the pamphlets of the Classic, Paul Louis Courier? Where will you find a more superb panorama of the world than in the *Mémoires* of the Romantic, Chateaubriand? But you will notice that Gourmont has ingeniously described two types of mind, which appear, and perhaps are, antithetical. The one sort of mind, which he calls Classic, always works outwards from itself; the other sort, which he calls Romantic, always plunges deeper and deeper into itself. The one is extensive, the other intensive. Now the remarkable thing about Gourmont's mind is that it did not belong exclusively to either of these types, but to both. His mind was both extensive and intensive. He was both Romantic and Classic. If ever a man plunged into his own mind, brooded introspectively and knew the utter boredom of introspection, that man was Remy de Gourmont. Read his poems, the poetical prose of his *Pélérin du Silence,* even his novels like the *Chevaux de Diomède.* There is a mind which has thought itself weary with introspection, a sensibility which has fed upon itself until it is exasperated to a more than Baudelairean boredom. Yet the same person, the same mind, found infinite entertainment in a variety of intellectual interests outside itself. The author of *Proses Moroses* and of *Perverse Litanies of Love* composed an essay on the "Philosophy of Happiness" and wrote, among other things, two series of sprightly dialogues on current events. You will agree that there is every reason to insist on the complexity of this man's mind; but do not hastily conclude that so much complexity implies nothing but incoherence, excessive instability or a kind of intellectual hypocrisy.

There is a well-known fairy-story of a little Princess who received many desirable gifts from her good fairy-godmothers; and then a wicked fairy-godmother added another gift which made them all useless. Well, Gourmont was rather like that. He was gifted in so many ways and he had not the gift of selecting which of his gifts he would develop and which he would abandon. He was a mixture of a Romantic artist—poet and novelist—and an eighteenth-century philosophe. Perhaps if he had resolutely stifled one of these halves of his dual self, the other might have had room to grow more freely. Was he, one asks, like those over-greedy gardeners who refuse to thin out their crops and consequently gather only a multitude of stunted plants which have mutually warred against each other? It is certain that even the most energetic mind gains by concentration, that intellectual curiosity when over-indulged ceases to be a virtue and becomes a vice. Who is to decide? So many factors are involved. You will find more essential information about the French Revolution in one of Lord Acton's essays than in all Carlyle's fervid fiction; yet the indispensable work on that event is still the huge, eight-volume history of Albert Sorel. The bust, says Gautier, survives the city. Yes, but we need re-builders of cities as much as fashioners of busts. We need interpreters of the "spirit of an age" as much as exclusive artists. By refusing to leave any part of his mind uncultivated, by using his mind in its totality, Gourmont attempted a great thing. He was, I believe, consciously or unconsciously, attempting to carry on French thought from the point it had reached—and that was a high point—at the time of the Revolution. Gourmont attempted to harmonize logical reason, experimental truth and sentiment or "intuition." He tried to unite in the flow of one personality the various streams of French intellectual and artistic life. It was, at any rate, a rather splendid failure.

Perhaps I can make this clearer by translating a passage from a new book on the eighteenth century by that eminent authority, M. Daniel Mornet:

The men of the end of the 18th century are infinitely nearer to those of the end of the 19th century than to those of the end of the 17th. We can say that they grasped all the forms of our contemporary thought, even that they perceived its consequences and contradictions. They carried the spirit of investigation, the rights of rational criticism to their extreme limits. If their idea of historical criticism and of reconstructing the past were not so clear and so methodical as that of the historians and exegisists of the 19th century, they at least understood the essential requirements and sketched out the methods. They saw with the greatest clearness that logical and abstract truth, the agreement of the mind with itself, geometrical and mathematical reasoning are a human construction and that they are not necessarily the whole truth nor even perhaps the truth. They understood, as clearly as our modern men of science, what constitutes experimental truth, the laws which are inductively derived from facts and experiment and not those which are deduced by abstract reasoning. Abstract systems, hypotheses, experimental laws—they saw how all these efforts at explanation complete or contradict

each other. At the same time they realized that reason and science would never include the whole of the universe. The unrol-
ling of rational and experimental truths carries us to infinity on
an endless road, a road which leads farther and farther away from
the truths necessary to life. However precise and numerous the
reasons of Reason and the laws of our sciences, they cannot give
us the explanation of our destiny, our reasons for acting, the
secret of happiness. We can only perceive these reasons and this
secret by the light of what they called "sentiment" and "the
heart," or, as we say, "intuition." Logical reason, experimental
truth, the intuition of the "heart," are the three forces which
occupy our modern thought and which we are perpetually trying
to order or to harmonize.

I suspect that M. Daniel Mornet would have us abandon
the endless road for the road to Rome; but that need not
concern us now. I quote the passage because I think it
explains what Gourmont instinctively and often hesitatingly
was trying to do. It gives a clue to his complexity, to the
apparent contradiction, over-subtlety and versatility we see in
his mind. French thought and literature are not new things.
The intellectual inheritance of a Frenchman is so large and
so complicated that he runs a serious risk of being overcome
by it. This, I think, is why so many young and some not so
young writers both in France and elsewhere have made a
virtue of ignorance, and wish to destroy all that has been
painfully garnered during so many centuries. In his young
days, Gourmont himself was infected by this Attis-worship.
But his mind was candid and his curiosity acute; he could
not help reading; having read, he was bound to admire, and
he was always ready to admit that a small increase of knowledge had chastened in him that spirit of sweeping condemnation which is so often the spirit of ignorance. If I may accept
M. Mornet's description as a fairly true account of the state
of thought in France, perhaps you will agree that it was a
useful thing for some men to combine in themselves "logical
reason, experimental truth and the intuitions of sentiment."

I do not wish to claim, or to seem to claim for Gourmont
a position higher than that justified by his published works. I
have called him a "modern man of letters" and only in that

comparatively humble status do I desire to rank him. I have
tried to describe a sort of mind which, I believe, was a good
type of mind produced by France in the second half of the
nineteenth century. Gourmont was a distinct but not unique
example of that type. He was not a great artist, not a great
philosopher, not a great critic. As a literary artist he is not to
be compared with Gustave Flaubert; as a personality, as
scholar and man of science, he is vastly inferior to Ernest
Renan; and as critic of literature and ideas, he comes behind
Sainte-Beuve. He was one of France's most able and indus-
trious journeymen of letters. But a literature is rich when it
can afford to rank such writers among its journeymen.
France has been fortunate in possessing many of these versa-
tile interpreters; they are useful at all times, but especially
important in a democracy. Let me give a practical demon-
stration: Twenty-five years ago France was agitated by wild
and incoherent ideas of social utopia, not unlike ourselves
today. These ideas were riddled with criticism by Gourmont
and others of his kind. Their arguments filtered from the
special reviews to wider audiences and even to the press; if a
serious danger were averted, this was in part due to the
superior journeymen of letters. The French public may be
misled as easily as any other; but it can be made to listen to
logical criticism.

I have said that Gourmont was gifted in many ways and
yet I have been compelled to rank him only as a skilled
journeyman. The explanation of this apparent paradox lies in
the fact that he found his maturity very late, almost too late.
Even a critic of ideas, even a very subtle-minded man, should
begin to know himself and his mind soon after thirty. Gourmont was nearly forty when he published the *Livre des
Masques*, the first book which showed his genuine capabili-
ties. He was forty-five when he obtained full possession of his
talent; and at fifty the best of his energy was spent. He
wasted far too many years in mere fumbling, far too many
years in the acquisition of abstruse learning while neglecting
more important studies, and far too many years in the pur-
suit of a factitious and affected originality. I attribute this
unlucky state of affairs to a genuine spirit of contradiction in

Gourmont himself and to the influence of Huysmans and Villiers de Lisle Adam.

It is good that both artist and critic should refuse to accept current values without examination, that they should resist the forces which always try to bend them to inferior service. But it is bad for either always to reject the opinion of a majority merely because it is a majority. Gourmont wilfully made himself "precious." He affected to prefer the Latin poets of the Middle Ages to the classics, not because he had made a profound study of Latin literature and had gradually come to make this startling reversal of judgment; but because it was a minority opinion, a fad of his friend, J. K. Huysmans. You may recollect the chapters in *A Rebours* where Huysmans not unamusingly denies the classics and exaggerates the value of medieval authors; and you may also have read the scathing article by Jules Lemaître—who knew what he was talking about—where he shows the absurdity of Huysmans' judgments. Huysmans was not a Latin scholar. He borrowed most of his information from a learned German. He had never read the authors he criticized so dogmatically. The young Gourmont was uncritical enough to be duped by Huysmans. He wasted much time in the vast folios of the Abbé Migne and produced a commented anthology of medieval Latin poetry, a book not without interest to an ordinary reader but one which is passed over with silent contempt by scholars. I give this as an example of the over-prolonged immaturity of Gourmont's mind. It took him much too long to extricate himself from this and other intellectual blind alleys. I am far from disparaging the study of medieval literature; I am only trying to show that Gourmont approached it in the wrong way and with the wrong spirit. In his conceit he even thought he had "discovered" works which are known to many theological students. And he did not even conclusively prove his one valid point—that these neglected poets do deserve to be studied as literature.

Huysmans and Villiers were both disappointed men. Nothing is more unfortunate for a young and inexperienced author than a strong influence from older authors who have failed, either as men or as artists. I have myself seen a writer of some promise ruined by an uncritical admiration and friendship for a disappointed senior who imbued the younger man with all his personal enmities, all his whims and fads, all his feelings of bitterness against the world. With the candor of youth, the young writer accepted discontented grumblings as sober facts; and, with the reckless generosity of youth, made this lost cause his own. Something of the kind happened to Gourmont in his friendship for Huysmans and Villiers. If he had thrown off their influence before thirty, no very great harm would have been done. But the influence lasted until he was nearly forty and, although he did eventually conquer his independence and attain his own originality, he was damaged by a perhaps regrettable association.

I have given one specific instance of Huysmans' influence on Gourmont. From this same unequal writer and very unamiable man, Gourmont acquired his youthful affectations of style and the querulous tone of his early criticism. We all enjoy discussion of art and literature and most of us enjoy an able pleading for unorthodox views. But no man, who has truly understood the lessons of humane letters, wishes to quarrel about them; and no man of spirit will allow himself to be sneered into admiring a novelty which does not please him. By adopting these methods the young Gourmont alienated sympathies from himself and from the cause he defended. What is admirable in him is that his good sense finally triumphed and that he learned at length to criticize as a man of letters, not as a querulous schoolboy.

From Villiers Gourmont acquired many of his questionable early tastes in literature. Villiers was an unsuccessful author, with a good deal more talent than he was then allowed. But he was a bigot, a fantastic, and utterly uncritical in any good sense, though he continually found fault with most things. Villiers initiated Gourmont into his own taste for flamboyant mysticism, his exaggerated application of the principles of subjective idealism, his admiration for the flowery portions of Poe's prose writings, and his hatred for all positive thought. As a result the young Gourmont accepted the opinions of a literary sect, when he thought he was defending a glorious new development of French literature. Much that one deplores in his work comes from this sectarian spirit. He was eventually saved from it by his intellectual curiosity, by his regard for truth and, probably, by the energetic influence of Nietzsche. The theory of the transvaluation of values must have been very welcome to a man who delighted to find as many sides to a question as possible.

I do not mean to reject the whole of Gourmont's work before 1898, nor do I mean to imply that his real attitude was completely insincere or that he abruptly changed. The Gourmont I now value is the mature Gourmont of *Promenades Philosophiques* and *Promenades Littéraires*, of the *Chemin de Velours*, of *La Culture des Idées* and of the *Dialogue des Amateurs*. The maturity of Gourmont really dates from the time when he at length learned the necessity for limitation, when he abandoned the hopeless ambition of knowing and experiencing everything. When he made that decision he tacitly gave his adhesion to the tradition of his race.

There is evolution in Gourmont's development and, vastly as he changed, there is no sudden break. Moreover, there was a basis of sincerity even in his affectations—by which I mean that they were at least consistent with his general attitude at the time. At most periods of his literary career he strove to harmonize logical reason, experimental truth and the intuitions of sentiment. Not unnaturally one or the other predominated at various times, and at different periods of his life they meant very different things to him. Take a cross section of his work in any epoch and you will find that in all its genres it is consistent. Similarly, there is a sort of consistency in his work as a whole, though the consistency is complex. The general trend of his advance from one position to another can be traced, but he wandered by all the side paths instead of taking the direct road.

He moved from the acceptance of the extreme consequences of subjective idealism, to a position where he could actually say that the essentials of philosophy were to be found in the French eighteenth century, and that the Germans from Kant to Schopenhauer had added only unnecessary metaphysical trimmings. That, as you may say, proves he was no philosopher. It certainly seems to prove that he was not much of a metaphysician. I am inclined to think that he accepted his subjective idealism on trust from Villiers and did not ever thoroughly comprehend it. I myself am not metaphysical. Subjective idealism irritates me as it irritated Dr. Johnson, and I must make the humiliating confession that I am not able to refute it any better than he. But you will see why I can more easily sympathize with the later than the earlier Gourmont.

As I have said, he was consistent at each stage of his journey. Let us look at him when he was the uncompromising subjective realist, when the universe was a creation of M. de Gourmont's consciousness. For him nothing existed except as he perceived it; consequently, nothing mattered to him except his perception. "A man knows only his own intelligence," wrote Gourmont in 1891, "only himself, the sole reality, his special and unique world . . . nothing occurs outside the perceptive subject; all I think is real; the sole reality is thought." What is the result of this doctrine? Politically it leads to anarchy, and Gourmont then professed a sort of dilettante anarchism. It leads to a denial of the validity of science, for science assumes that there is something objective to be known. And Gourmont at that time spoke scornfully of science. In its place, he entertained a vague mysticism, a vague religiosity. The only standard of criticism, either of literature or ideas, was his own subjective impression. Villiers was greater than Voltaire, Mallarmé superior to Molière, because Gourmont happened to "perceive" so at the moment of writing. Even writing itself was solely for his own satisfaction; it was a purely subjective entertainment. (Whether the publication was also purely subjective, he did not stop to inquire.) Applied to creative literature the idea was also fertile. Poetry need have no meaning except for the poet himself, and consequently Gourmont crooned long and sometimes melodious "litanies" which have no particular meaning. The novel naturally could not reproduce a non-existent objective world and so it became the cerebral adventures of M. de Gourmont. Small wonder he was bored. To appreciate his escape, you must recollect that a large number of Gourmont's contemporaries remained permanently lost in the mist. Whether Gourmont ever disposed of his metaphysical problem I do not know. He made two or three fruitless attempts, and then decided, like Voltaire before him, that metaphysics are vain, "the art of reasoning about that which we do not know." At all events he abandoned his "precious" manner. Nietzsche or his own common sense shocked him out of his religiosity, which was never a spiritual conviction but merely an affectation of vestments, incense, and plain-song. He became interested in biology and physics, in the study of grammar and philology; his essays making known recent discoveries and his own ideas about them attracted attention. He ceased to be bored; he ceased to argue that his own small literary set held a monopoly of talent; he returned from Gotteschalkus to Lucretius, from Hello to Renan, from Huysmans to Sainte-Beuve. He composed his essay on the philosophy of happiness and planned that panegyric of the classic mind I quoted earlier. The Voltairean who dwells somewhere in every Frenchman came to the surface. He was witty where formerly he had only sneered, and instead of a monstrous interest in his own "Perceptive subject" he found interest in the intellectual life going on about him. In place of the "cerebral adventures" of his novel *Sixtine*, he produced *Une Nuit au Luxembourg*, a pagan version of Christianity which would have made Voltaire's wig stand on end, and, except under the tolerance of the Third Republic, would have led either to prison or the stake. He earnestly defended the Jesuits on the paradoxical grounds that they were the least Christian of all Christians; and, which is still more remarkable, he brought evidence to prove the point. If there is still excess here, it comes from too ruthless a devotion to logical reason, a devotion only completely admirable in monks and scientific specialists. In life and in art, in politics and in morals, logical reason must always be tempered by the intuitions of sentiment. Perhaps if some woman had firmly taken charge of him when he was thirty he would not have been so logical, so terribly logical.

I am unwilling to leave the subject of Remy de Gourmont

merely with these generalities. I should like to put before you a few of his ideas which at various times have interested me. Perhaps the most ambitious among these are the theory of the dissociation of ideas and the idea of a law of an intellectual constant. Neither of these is wholly original. For example, Keats played with the idea of a law of an intellectual constant in his letter to Rice, of the 25th March, 1818. Dissociation of ideas is a purely logical process. Probably it was suggested to Gourmont by his reading among medieval schoolmen or, still more likely, by the Jesuit casuists. It is really a process of drawing subtle distinctions, but with it is that modern desire for accuracy of thought and expression which has prompted a recent book on the Meaning of Meaning.

Gourmont expounds his theory of the dissociation of ideas as follows:

There are two ways of thinking. Either you accept ideas and associations of ideas as they are in general use, or, on your own account you form new associations and, which is rarer, original dissociations of ideas. You imagine new relations between old ideas and old images; or you separate old ideas and old images united by tradition, examine them one by one, even if you re-form them into an infinity of new combinations which may again be split up. In the field of facts and experiment these operations are limited by the resistance of matter and the law of physics; in the purely intellectual field they must submit to logic; but since logic itself is an intellectual structure it is almost infinitely obliging . . .

Some associations of ideas are so durable that they appear eternal . . . They are usually called "commonplace." . . . A commonplace is something more and something less than a banality; it is a banality but sometimes unavoidable; it is a banality but so universally accepted that it is called a truth. Most truths which fly about the world may be considered as commonplaces, that is, associations of ideas common to a great many men and such that hardly one of these men would dare to break intentionally. Man, in spite of his tendency towards mendacity, has a great respect for what he calls truth; truth is his travelling staff in life, commonplaces are the bread in his scrip, the wine in his bottle. Deprived of commonplaces, men would find themselves defenceless, helpless and without food. They need truths so much that they adopt new truths without abandoning old truths, and so the mind of a civilized man is a museum of contradictory truths.

A few analytical minds have attempted in vain to draw up an inventory of their contradictions; to each objection of reason, sentiment immediately finds a good excuse, for sentiments, as M. Ribot has shown, are the strongest things in us and represent permanence and continuity.

Man associates ideas not according to logic, according to verifiable exactitude, but according to his pleasure and his interest. And consequently many truths are nothing but prejudices.

I trust I have not made the theory incoherent and incomprehensible by trying to compress it. What he means is that there are numbers of ideas floating about in peoples' minds, vague, general ideas, like the idea of justice, the idea of truth, the idea of honor, the idea of an idea, and so on. Unquestionably, these ideas have a considerable influence on human conduct. By dissociating them, Gourmont meant an attempt to analyze them into their true, not their conventional elements. It is really an attempt to discover the Meaning of Meaning. Let me give one brief example of this method in practice. Gourmont says:

The idea of liberty as presented to us by politicians is one of these incoherences. When we hear the word we hardly understand anything except political liberty, and yet it appears as if all the liberties a civilized man can enjoy are contained in this ambiguous expression. The pure idea of liberty is like the pure idea of justice; it can be of no use to us in the ordinary business of life. Neither man nor Nature is free, any more than man and Nature are just. Reasoning has no hold on such ideas. To express them is to assert them, but they would necessarily falsify every argument into which they were brought. Reduced to its social sense, the idea of liberty is still imperfectly dissociated; there is no general idea of it and it is hard to form one, since the liberty of an individual is only exerted at the expense of the liberty of others. At one time liberty was called Privilege, and that perhaps is its true name; even today, one of our relative liberties, the liberty of the press, is a collection of privileges; the liberty of speech granted to advocates is also privilege; so is the liberty of trades unions.

In the course of my duties as a servant of the press, I am frequently called upon to judge books and novels by young men and women—and old ones too—which offer a distracted world the one and infallible recipe for salvation. These infallible recipes are surprisingly various. Lady novelists are usually in favor of Love, Love with a large *L* for the cosmos, and love with a small *l* for the erring but amiable hero. Others think that all will be well if only we can identify the "I" with the "not I." Some advocate practical measures: the abolition of all machines, or the abolition of the Renaissance, or the destruction of libraries and professors, or the unlimited fabrication of paper money. I have even been forced to read a book which hinted that the world would be saved if only the great merchants of London and the North of England could be made to believe in fairy tales; and the book was not written by a company promoter. Recently the word has gone forth that the world is to be saved by abolishing democracy and setting up a new autocracy. You and I and the rest of the herd are to be sternly reduced to our proper spheres of insignificance, while these paper autocrats receive the glories of the Pharaohs and the Ming dynasty. It needs no spirit from the vasty deep to tell us that all these alleged ideas are fudge. Still, a candid and guileless mind might have its doubts. To resolve them, apply Gourmont's method of dissociation. It is warranted to analyze almost any chimera into its original element of tepid air.

Instead of describing Gourmont's theory of the law of an intellectual constant, which is perhaps a little arid, let me quote a page of his literary criticism and a few of the numerous aphorisms I have marked in his books. He says of Herbert Spencer:

The glory of Spencer is that he brought the idea of evolution into general philosophy. If he did not invent this idea, he clarified it, perhaps excessively, and gave it at least a very great dialectical value. It is an old idea, a primitive idea, the normal idea by which men naturally explain the present universe. Lamarck first gave it a concrete form; it is the basis of his zoölogical philosophy. Then Lyell contributed geology to it. Then came Spencer who tried to bend to it the whole world of phenomena.

The philosophers before Socrates and Plato are quite clearly evolutionists. The recent notion that terrestrial fauna derive from marine fauna is advanced by Anaximander who, moreover, enlarged the idea of evolution to include the sidereal world. Plato and the Christians destroyed Science, which had to be reconquered bit by bit by constant effort, perpetually hindered by theological despotism, which is even more dangerous, because of the mask of intellectual illusion it puts on to seduce simple and candid minds.

Spencer, then, links up across the centuries ancient and modern science. Had he realized this, his optimism would no doubt have dwindled to modest proportions, for, instead of thinking of progress as a straight line, he would have sent it passing into the future in chance curves which might just as easily lead to retrogression as to expansion. If his mind dwelt on these contradictions, it was only for a moment. He lacked the courage to look the sphinx steadily in the eyes, to conceive a blind, indifferent, strictly material, evolution, stripped of all sentimental, hedonist, progressivist and humanitarian frippery. He never rose to the height where the point of view is purely scientific; evolution must satisfy his heart, be beneficient, have as its object Man, his moralization, his happiness. He dreamed in all seriousness of a happy race of men, simmering in the joy of life, like a weevil in flour. Herbert Spencer is even more responsible than Comte for the idea of a paradisical finality, which men today dream of stupidly for a remote posterity, which doubtless will scorn their folly.

Gourmont wrote of Voltaire:

After having detested almost everything in Voltaire, I have come to like almost everything. As I read him, I came to see that he was not only a great writer, but a wise man. What he praised, deserved to be praised, what he derided, deserved contempt. He is, I think, the surest mind I have ever known, and, in spite of what the fools say, the least superficial. He talked about everything because he knew everything. Read him, Voltaire is a perpetual surprise.

Here are some of his aphorisms:

(1) La Rochefoucauld made men more cunning than they are. He placed his wit at the service of humanity.

(2) Social revolutionaries make me think of a man whose piano is out of tune, who says: "Let us smash up this piano and

throw its pieces in the fire; and then we'll install an Aeolian harp."

(3) The altruist is an unreasonable egoist; he wants all men to be modelled on his own sensibility.

(4) Not only is the soul not immortal, but it is the one thing that is mortal. A man perishes: the elements of his body survive and are transformed: his mind disappears.

(5) I have often written the word "Beauty," but hardly ever without realizing that I was writing nonsense. There are beautiful objects, but no such thing as Beauty: it is an abridged expression. It cannot be taken as an absolute; there is no absolute.

(6) Posterity is like a schoolboy condemned to learn a hundred lines of verse by heart. He remembers ten, and stammers a few syllables of the rest. The ten lines are fame; the rest is literary history.

2

Aldous Huxley

I have to confess my ignorance, as one so often has to do. I have not followed Mr. Huxley's work closely; and this seems ridiculous, since I find myself so much in sympathy with him and admire what I have read of his so much. In 1919 and 1920 I think I read everything he wrote; and I have always maintained that his poetry is estimated far below its real worth. But between 1920 and *Point Counter Point* I admit with shame that I read nothing of his—an omission I intend to repair. It was entirely my fault or misfortune. For reasons not unconnected with the War, I turned away from modern literature (except certain sections of it) and plunged into a gluttonous reading of other ages. So I come to *Do What You Will* with a particularly open mind. Perhaps that is why I like it so much.

In *Do What You Will* Mr. Huxley has said a great many things extremely worth saying, things I should have liked to say myself if I had his ability. I don't agree with all he says, and I think he might be attacked successfully along certain lines, but I prefer to write about what I like and admire in his book.

The most important thing I admire is Mr. Huxley's valiant, and I believe successful, attempt to say something positive, to set up a sanction for life. I am sick of death and death worshipping in all its forms, from senile gentility to the cold butchery of intellectual suicide. Let me give an example. A greatly admired poem by the most admired poet of the day may be summarized in the following excerpted words:

Article published in the *Sunday Referee*, London, 15 December 1929.

Hollow—dried—meaningless—dry—broken—dry—paralysed—
death's—hollow—I dare not—death's—broken—fading—death's
—final—twilight—dead—cactus—stone—dead—fading—death's
—broken—dying—broken—last—sightless—death . . .

The poet's genius is not in question, but I hate this
exhibitionism of a perpetual suicidal mania which never,
never, comes to the point. If that's all there is to life, why
not go off with a revolver bang, instead of endlessly whimper-
ing? Besides, the attitude is past, out of date. It is the War
despair which involved so many of us and from which the
healthy-minded have been struggling to escape, not yearning
to wallow in. Mr. Huxley has struggled tremendously and
bravely, and I think he has escaped. He has got back to a
positive belief in life, a positive enjoyment of life. And he
has not done it by yielding to the old nauseating humbugs,
the false official optimisms which are like a bad but insipid
smell. Perhaps Mr. Huxley's escape is only valid for himself
and for a few who by education and temperament are predisposed to sympathy with him, but at least he has found a way
to life—that's something.

A life-worshipper, so Mr. Huxley describes himself. One
up to him! With all the various forms of death and death-
worship now popular, real courage is needed to take up such
a position and great skill to defend it successfully. But what
is meant by "life"? (The question must be asked with a
would-be-superior sneer.) Well, I think Mr. Huxley has answered the question by the whole of his book, which should
be read by everyone who is interested in our life here and
now. But he has also answered it in a very quotable passage,
which may stand as a definition of what he means by "life":

Man has a mind: very well, let him think. Senses that enjoy:
let him be sensual. Instincts: they are there to be satisfied.
Passions: it does a man good to succumb to them from time to
time. Imagination, a feeling for beauty, a sense of awe: let him
create, let him surround himself with lovely forms, let him
worship. Man is multifarious, inconsistent, self-contradictory;
the Greeks accepted the fact and lived multifariously, incon-
sistently and contradictorily. Their polytheism gave divine sanction to this realistic acceptance. "All the Gods ought to have

praise given to them." There was therefore no need for remorse or the consciousness of sin.

By one of those pleasing coincidences which sometimes happen in life, I received Mr. Huxley's book after a day spent in Pompeii. All the way back I had been thinking, not of Bulwer Lytton's absurd and mythical Roman sentry, but of the past life whose ghost has been imprisoned there for us by the volcano. Heaven knows, Pompeii was a common little provincial town, a kind of Southend. But it keeps a pleasant fragrance of pre-Christian European life. While I was still trying to find words to express the impression it gives my eyes chanced on the passage I have just quoted. That is it. There was still enough Hellenism in that small Campanian town for the inhabitants to wish to be men, and not gods or devils.

I am not setting up the Pompeians as ideal people, and I don't mean to play the easy game of attributing to the past the virtues or qualities neither it nor we possess. But I do think that we can live out our own lives fully as human beings, just as those Romanized Hellenes and Oscans and Samites of Pompeii seem to have done. I think that is the gist of what Mr. Huxley says so cogently (and often wittily) in these essays. His conviction that we must live here and now dictated his admirable analysis of monotheism, his exposition of the diversity of the human being, his ruthless exposure (how I welcomed it!) of the slobbered-over Francis of Assisi, his twenty-six rounds with Pascal—the best onslaught upon that formidable "death-worshipper" I have read since Voltaire's. Further, Mr. Huxley's exposition of how the effort to live in a superhuman fashion inevitably results in sub-human compensations seems to me both convincing and valuable. It shows you exactly why the Unco Guid are such ruthless persecutors and tormentors. His dislike for all unbalanced and cock-eyed living is very cordial. Even his analysis of Dostoievsky's characters (perhaps a little unfair) I greeted with a mild cheer—I am very sick of the Russian idiot-Christ.

At times I have meditated a modest apologue, based on the theory of the transmigration of souls, where a man spends each of his innumerable lives in maceration and misery, preparing himself to enjoy felicity in his next life and always finding it was quite different from what he had expected. One life at a time. The problem, as Mr. Huxley puts it, is for us worms to be the best of all possible worms. No self-maiming, either in the interests of Paradise or big business. The one objection I find to Mr. Huxley's philosophy of life is this. It is a most attractive, if difficult, programme, but it is infinitely easier for him and for me (who live on the margin of the commercial-industrial world as its spoiled amusers) than for those, the great majority, who have to live that life. Halcott Glover once said to me: "No man who has managed to keep out of an office can be called a failure in life." All well and good, but most men don't manage it. Most men *are* in offices or factories or industrial jobs of some sort. If they all took up their beds and followed Mr. Huxley he and I would be reduced to mendicants in a few months. "Life" cannot be the monopoly of a few intelligent upper middle-class people and artists. To do Mr. Huxley justice, he makes a strong effort to deal with this in his essay called "Revolutions." But that is extremely pessimistic in its conclusions. "It will be a Nihilist revolution. Destruction for destruction's sake. Hate, universal hate, and an aimless and therefore complete and thorough smashing up of everything."

Most depressing, and I don't believe it. Here Mr. Huxley is a little inhuman, as he is in his attack on the talkies and movies—attacking them from the basis of the world's worst film (Al Jolson's beastly Mammy sentimentalism) seen in Paris, where there has been a trade blockade for months of American films, where German and Russian films appear ruthlessly cut, where the native producers seem to me mostly imbeciles, who have never grasped the elements of film production. (If you are ever tempted to go to a Jean Epstein film, don't.) The movies are part of the life of our time, and I refuse to clip that little head from my hydra because Mr. Huxley objects to the merchants of film production. I might just as well object to his book because it is printed by a machine and not exquisitely calligraphed by hand. The camera can produce results as surprising and beautiful as those of paint and brushes. If Mr. Huxley disbelieves this, let him go and see what Mr. Man Ray can do. Besides, the mere rhythm of action and vitality in films like *Tempest over Asia* and *The Mad Czar* is enough to refute Mr. Huxley's criticisms—or prejudices.

3

Wyndham Lewis

This latest novel of Mr. Lewis's presents us with such a problem in literary criticism that it is impossible to avoid rushing in at once with an opinion. Its bulk invites comparison with the early editions of *Ulysses*. Like *Ulysses*, it is episodic and not narrative. But there the resemblance halts. Mr. Joyce affects impartiality toward his characters, whereas Mr. Lewis makes no effort at all to conceal the cold ferocity of his hatred for the society he attacks.

The Apes of God is one of the most belligerent books I have ever read. Its perpetual stream of satire rolls like drumfire and the bayonets of Mr. Lewis's attacking divisions gleam between the lines. No quarter is asked or given, and the resulting massacre of the innocents is truly hair-raising. When you consider the prodigal exertion of energy and its victims, you are inevitably reminded of the god Thor using his invincible hammer to crack monkey nuts. In fact, the whole thing is overdone. While the reader is fascinated into admiration by Mr. Lewis's gifts as a writer, his energy, his wit, his style, his tremendous gusto, his ferocious sense of farce, the attack is made with such frightfulness and the victims are so comparatively innocent that all sympathy is diverted to the casualties which are caused by this Lewis Gun of Literature. 'Tis excellent to have a giant's strength, but —

The Apes of God, though one of the cruelest, is also one of the most tremendous farces ever conceived in the mind of man. For comparisons one must fall back on Rabelais and Aristophanes. Pope and Voltaire are gently urbane after Mr.

Two articles published in the *Sunday Referee*, London, 15 and 22 June, 1930.

Lewis. They were armed with old-fashioned muzzle-loaders, whereas he employs every known device of modern warfare. Everything about the book is on a huge scale. The characters are all well over life-size, physical giants who tramp and crash about the scene, presumably to atone for their otherwise harmless insignificance. These farcical Rouault figures are evoked only to be massacred, and the stage at the end is more littered with broken bodies than in the bloodiest of Elizabethan tragedies of blood. It is the most impressive display of Schrecklichkeit ever witnessed in literature.

But why, one asks, waste all this tremendous energy, wit, and hatred on a set of Bloomsbury and Chelsea parish pumpers? Why, in fact, be so confoundedly literary in one's hates? Why launch Achilles into a Batrachomiomachia? Even if you make the frogs and mice nine feet high? Hit those your own size! What have the unlucky X, Y, and Z done that they should thus be sent festering through Florence? Well, it appears that most of them have private incomes and have published books or exhibited pictures which Mr. Lewis dislikes. He thinks they are childish, both art and artists. "Immersed in the make-believe of the adult nursery, described in *The Art of Being Ruled*, all have become 'irresponsible baby-boys and baby-girls,' in the same way that the French Court, in the days before the Revolution, dressed themselves as shepherds and shepherdesses in their *fêtes champêtres*." All right, and probably true. But, in the first place, did not the ruling classes of the virile Renaissance dress up as Pans and Echoes, did not Le Roi Soleil himself —emblem of all good order and discipline—play exactly similar games in a solemn classical style at Versailles; and, in the second place, does one throw bombs at naughty or silly children?

Mr. Lewis wastes incalculable treasures of intellectual brilliance in satirizing an amateur publisher and the goings-on of three aristocratic poets. He claims that such people reflect "the collapse of English social life in the grip of Post-War conditions." *Que nenni*. In an industrial community ruled by plutocrats Mr. Lewis's victims are the merest side-show. I would wager that thirty-nine and a half millions of the forty

millions of people in our country have never even heard of
the kind of person Mr. Lewis attacks, and that not 5 percent
of the remaining half million cares enough about them even
to take his broadest points. Even within those narrow limits
a further inconvenience results. A type of writer and artist,
more pernicious than those Mr. Lewis slaughters, the os-
trich-like defenders of dead nineteenth-century tradition, will
be emboldened by his genius to lift a diminished head and
add still further to the general confusion. It is as if in the
France of 1890 Mr. Lewis had triumphantly downed, say,
Régnier, Samain, and Pierre Louys (undoubtedly vulnerable
to attack) with the quite unexpected result of benefiting
Sully-Prudhomme, Georges Ohnet, and the manes of Hugo.
In other words, why act as a super-Nordau and encourage the
cricketers of literature?

There remain untouched by all this the quality of Mr.
Lewis's intellect and the quality of his writing. He is wholly
distrustful of all feelings and emotions—in this the complete
antithesis of Lawrence—and he is an amazing example of the
power and limitations of pure intelligence. *The Apes of God*
is produced by the intellect for the intellect. Its passions,
which are almost exclusively those of hatred and contempt,
are intellectual passions. Its method is destructive analysis.
Behind the pages lurks the mysterious presence of the super-
intellectual Pierpoint, who, as it were, directs all the strategy
of the campaign. Zagreus, a homosexual Greek, is one of the
disciples of Pierpoint, and undertakes to initiate an enormous Irish moron, named Dan, into the mysteries of the Ape
world. (Why Mr. Lewis lavishes this highly complicated
education on so unreceptive a moron is perhaps only one
more example of his prodigious contempt for mankind—
there is no one else!)

Thereafter the book becomes a new *Candide*, and the
luckless Dan is dragged uncomprehending from one den of
Apes to another, ending up with an enormous country-house
agape of the intelligentsia. All this having achieved nothing
but slaughter, Mr. Lewis sardonically betroths Zagreus to a
homicidal but senile aristocrat, who expires with emotion at
the first kiss. You have the feeling that Mr. Lewis would like

to kill anybody, old or young, who enjoyed anything so glandular as a mere kiss.

But there can be no doubt whatever of the prodigious power of Mr. Lewis's intellect and of the force and wit of his writing. While the novel is undoubtedly too long, too intricate, and too much concerned with elaborate destruction of ideas, it contains some of the most brilliant satirical writing ever committed to paper. As one example of a "portrait" of unparalleled virulence and wit, I should choose the first description of Ratner, "the Split-Man," which is afterwards spoiled by over-elaboration. As an example of superb farce, unimpeded by intellectual broadcasting, I should choose the scene where the unfortunate Dan finds himself acting as model to a very masculine lady painter. Dan himself is a magnificent caricature of the post-War Sissy boy whose complete uselessness, timidity, and incompetence are only faintly excused by a kind of degenerate "niceness." My final feeling is that *The Apes of God* is the greatest piece of *writing* since *Ulysses,* and that with subjects more universal and less personal Mr. Lewis could produce a series of magnificent novels.

The literary weekly, *Everyman,* has recently published a very interesting interview with Mr. Wyndham Lewis on the subject of his new book, *The Apes of God.* Part of the interview was devoted to comments on my review of the book in the *Sunday Referee,* and I feel that either Mr. Lewis or his interviewer has misunderstood my point of view. Now I am particularly anxious that Mr. Lewis should not feel that I am against him, because essentially I am with him; and I feel that the artistic importance of *The Apes of God* justifies the abnormal procedure of devoting another article to it. I admire Mr. Lewis greatly, and I think *The Apes of God* a most remarkable and original novel. I said in my review that I thought it "the greatest piece of writing since *Ulysses,*" and I meant that to imply very great praise. Mr. Lewis has criticized *Ulysses* and so have I; and if I venture to make some reservations about *The Apes of God* the reason is that I think Mr. Lewis occupies a very important place in modern

English literature, both as a critic and as a creative artist. But I dare to think that such a position implies responsibilities, and if I venture to exhort Mr. Lewis it is with humility and because I believe him to be by far the more effective and gifted champion of our joint cause.

The cowardice which is characteristic of the dominant type of mind in England camouflages itself as "good taste," "good form," "a sense of humour," "the sporting spirit," and similar forms of cant. Mr. Lewis, on the contrary, has superb intellectual courage. He has shown that in this generation at least the English artist must fight with the gloves off, and if he can get hold of a few knuckle-dusters, so much the better. Mr. Lewis is the intellectual St. George of our rather un-merry England. *The Apes of God* is a great display of ferocious knight-errantry, but I was disappointed that our St. George came home with a bag of lizards and worms, instead of one or more of the numerous dragons which infest the landscape.

I suggested in my review that Mr. Lewis's victims are, on the whole, insignificant, and that he exaggerates their influence on the nation. This he counters by assimilating his Art Apes to the Communist Party in Russia, and by asserting that the Apes *do* influence the nation at large through the gossip columns of the dailies. The analogy is obviously strained. The Russian Communist Party is a stern set of political Ironsides, disciplined and organized, possessed of great political and military power, as well as the control of economic policy, in their own country. When Stalin says turn, they all turn. Mr. Lewis cannot expect us to believe that the puny, spiritless, unorganized, undisciplined Apes of Chelsea and Bloomsbury have any such power, or can brow-beat him, me, or the public. Where is the O.G.P.U. of the Apes? Whom have they shot in the neck? Where is their Lenin?

The Gossip Column argument is more specious, and I should be the last to deny that Mr. and Mrs. and Miss and Lord and Lady Gossip-Column degrade the intelligence of their readers. But is it really a fact that the Gossip Columns are to any great extent occupied with the sayings and doings of writers and painters, whether Apes or not, with the conse-

quence that Apery infects His Majesty's lieges at large?
(Nearly all Mr. Lewis's Apes are false writers and painters.)
I cannot claim to be an attentive reader of Gossip Columns,
but my impression is that they chiefly go in for the aristocracy and plutocracy, especially of the sporting kind, and their
stage partners in life—"Lord P. . . . tells me that he has
taken a million acre grouse shoot for the glorious twelfth;
Lady P. . . . , his lovely and talented wife, is famous for her
cocktail rags. She was, of course, known to a wide circle of
admirers before her marriage as Betty Binks, of the Lolly
Girls chorus." The stage, both film and board, easily out-
weighs every other sort of artist in the Gossip Columns; but
Mr. Lewis has practically spared the cabotins who are seen,
known, and heard by millions who never look at a picture
and rarely read a book. London hostesses, débutantes, polo
and tennis players, motorists and aviators, racing "mag-
nates," gas, light, and coal kings and queens, female M.P.'s,
owners of Riviera palaces, and Lido beach pyjamas, and the
like, are the fodder of the Gossipist. The writer and painter,
however apish, come far behind. The artist isn't news.

But, urges Mr. Lewis, this international Bohemia of the
Gossipist is precisely what I am attacking; these are the Apes,
these are the cretins who have cabbaged the arts to their
extreme detriment and the mental degradation of England.
This is where I disagree. In the first place, Mr. Lewis has
only attacked an unimportant aspect of the champagne Bohemia. His Lord Osmund got into the Gossip Columns because he was a lord, and not because he was a painter or
writer. Quite so, says Mr. Lewis, that's what I object to. And
I say: "Does it really matter?" Who really is duped by the
silly sycophancy of all this? Further, if Mr. Lewis would
study the owners of beach pyjamas and racehorses in their
own haunts, I believe he would find that they are totally
indifferent to all forms of art and literature—apish or not. In
fact, when they know anything about them, they despise the
Apes as much as Mr. Lewis—from below instead of from
above. If the majority of them knew a Bougereau from a
Picasso, or ever read anything more recondite than Edgar
Wallace and the newspaper, call me a shotten herring.

Let us assume for a moment that Mr. Lewis's Ratner is

alive and functioning. What the devil influence could that peddling personality have in corrupting England, or, indeed, anyone but a few footling women? Does Mayfair concern itself with Ratner, directly or indirectly? Does Westminster? Does the City? Do the suburbs? Do Manchester, Birmingham, Burnley, Newcastle, Sheffield, Bradford? Is Ratner discussed at Hendon, Brooklands, or Lord's? Hobbs has more fans than all the Apes united and quadrupled; "Chelsea" to England is a football team, and Bloomsbury's fame is sunk in that of the Tottenham Hotspurs.

The real dragons meanwhile remain regrettably unmolested. I shall not specify who and what they are. A truly independent paper like the *Sunday Referee* has enough enemies without having more pushed on it by its literary reviewers. But there is plenty of big game for Mr. Lewis. To attack there with all the force, wit, and ferocity of *The Apes of God* would indeed be a perilous and godlike task, and our St. George might meet a Waterloo. Nevertheless, the order should be, "Faites donner La Garde!" If he went down, it would be against a real and general foe, not a private and comparatively insignificant one.

It ill befits, as they say, the translator of M. Benda to throw bricks at him, but I do think Mr. Lewis overestimates the importance of *Belphégor*. M. Benda has one valid and important idea—*la trahison des clercs*, or the great treason of the intellectuals in putting their minds and influence to the service of Nationalism and Militarism—and this idea he has expanded with fastidious minuteness and elaboration. *Au fond*, M. Benda is an intellectualist pedant, dry as a stick and unimaginative as a pickled hambone. I imagine his *beau idéal* of great art would be a treatise by Renouvier or Pascal's *Lettres Provinciales* or something equally diverting and alive. His artistic sensibilities are about as lively as those of an Emeritus Professor of Higher Mathematics. I feel he would be gravely scandalized by all the vivid wit and imagination of *Blast* or *The Apes of God*.

I repeat, what I write here is in no sense an "attack" on Mr. Lewis. It is because I feel myself essentially with him that I want to see his genius not only working at its highest capacity but engaged on subjects worthy of him. Rabelais attacked fools and pedants, but he went chiefly after higher and more dangerous prey. I like to think of *The Apes of God* as a prologue to a great series of satires, which I feel sure Mr. Lewis can write. Perhaps he is already engaged on them. Fundamentally, our one difference here is that I think Mr. Lewis is pulling the fags' ears when he should be squaring up to the sixth-form bullies. Of course, if he says: "Now, my lad, straight out with it, are you for me or for the Apes?" my answer is, "For you, all the time and all the way; but don't be offended if I suggest that you're an International Heavy-weight, not a local gymnasium bantam."

4

Somerset Maugham

In literature success has its penalties no less than failure, though doubtless it is easier to bear the former with philosophic calm. Somerset Maugham has been and still is [written in 1939] one of the most consistently successful authors of his time; and at the same time he has almost stubbornly maintained his own point of view toward life and his slightly austere integrity as an artist. His attitude toward life is the not especially popular one of truth-seeker and truth-teller, and his method as an artist is the exacting one of unadorned and uncompromising precision and clarity. In Maugham you will find none of those soft, comforting half-truths so eagerly snatched at by an uncritical public; none of those purple passages of eloquence which are aimed more at the viscera than at the brain; none of the pretentious vagueness which so easily passes as profundity. With an art as unflattering to human weaknesses as Stendhal's he has succeeded in attracting far more than Stendhal's "happy few."

Now, on the face of it, you would think that here was a situation exactly made for those "serious critics," who, in their own rather unctuous phrase, "are concerned to maintain the standards of contemporary literature." How do they explain the persistent popular success of a writer who never flatters his audience, never compromises with the truth as he sees it, never plays stylistic tricks and remains quite indifferent to the ins and outs of literary fashion? They haven't attempted to do so. Dazzled and possibly a bit annoyed by the success, they have seen nothing else, and hastily and erroneously conclude that a writer who has continued to

First published as a pamphlet under the title W. *Somerset Maugham, An Appreciation* (New York: Doubleday, Doran & Co., Inc., 1939).

delight large audiences all over the world for several decades must be ephemeral and in some unspecified way unworthy of "serious consideration." Maugham has either been ignored or condescended to in a manner I find quite infuriating. What perverse nonsense it is to assume that a book or play which is immediately successful on a large scale must be bad! How more than vulgar to assume that because a writer makes no parade of "culture," he must therefore be uncultivated! My own impression is that Maugham knows more about literature, philosophy, and painting, and has better taste, than his condescending critics.

It is a great error on the part of the critics to suppose that a writer is uncultivated because he does not chatter the aesthetic jargon of the epoch and parrot the sayings of one or two intellectualist clique-leaders. A really cultivated man like Maugham reads and judges for himself. When Maugham writes criticism (as in *The Summing Up* and the preface to his *Collected Short Stories*) he is both interesting and acute. His remarks on Chekhov and Maupassant, for example, are wholly admirable. (I wish he would write more criticism—it is rare and so pleasant to come across a critic who is quite free from the offensive mannerisms of the professional book-harpies.)

But it is an even greater error to suppose that "culture" is any indication of a writer's ability to produce good plays, stories, and novels. Nobody ever went to a play because the author was an expert on Baroque architecture or got excited about a novelist because he knew Greek. Vastly more to the point is a wide and extensive knowledge of human beings, a genuine interest in them for their own sake. Here, I think, we come to the first reason for Maugham's success as a writer. He is greatly gifted both as an unconscious and a conscious observer of human beings, and he possesses an exact and vivid memory. Maugham is naturally a shy man, and the shy man's instinctive wish to avoid his fellow creatures could only have been broken down by an even greater interest in them and passion for the art of presenting them in words.

I once heard a pretentious high-brow say languidly that he

couldn't read Maugham, "because he always writes about the bourgeoisie." This person, I may say, was the author of much-discussed and much-praised works of criticism and supposed to be quite a literary dictator in his way. But what an absurd remark! If you are going to write about living human beings, how on earth can you ignore one of the largest and most important groups? And in Maugham's case it simply isn't true. In *The Moon and Sixpence* he has produced a vivid and convincing picture of the artist who will sacrifice everything for the sake of art. (Incidentally, the popular success of that book is one of Maugham's triumphs. It would be difficult to imagine a more "unpleasant" and "unpopular" character than Strickland, who occupies the whole center of the book. Yet by sheer mastery of his art Maugham compelled multitudes of readers to find matter for entertainment in the impossible Strickland.)

Again, in *Cakes and Ale*, there is the most amusing "private life" of the writer who from a shabby and disreputable past became a Grand Old Man of English letters, merely because he lived to a great age and had a second wife and a literary Egeria who were experts in dissimulation and intrigue. The same book contains a ruthless exposure of the successful literary faker of our own time, so true and so vivid that Alroy Kear becomes a living symbol of the whole literary racket in London.

Here, offhand, are three non-bourgeois characters. *Of Human Bondage*, with its astonishing profusion of characters, will alone furnish many more. Think of Mildred, the waitress, who inspires Philip with so disastrous a passion; the poor little hack-writer and super, Norah, who consoles him; Sally at the hop-picking; and then the working-class people Philip gets to know as a doctor. In the same book there are clear-cut sketches of the Paris Bohemians, Lawson, Clutton, Cronshaw, Miss Price. And, not to multiply examples from other books, only remember Maugham's portraits of Chinese and Malays, and the riff-raff of the East like Ginger Ted and the superbly vulgar prostitute in *Rain*. And this is the author who, according to a critic of allegedly international status, "always writes about the bourgeoisie" and therefore is not an artist!

A lot of humbug is being published now about the working class both by "proletarian" authors and by "socially
conscious" sympathizers, who seem agreed that art consists
of systematic falsification of truth for political purposes.
False presentation, asking for false compassion and indignation, can arouse little but contempt in a discerning reader.
Maugham's approach is entirely different. *Of Human Bondage* presents incidentally a picture of working class characters as they really are, with all their imperfections. But
Maugham does not fail to ask for and obtain deep compassion when the moment comes. I know very few incidents in
fiction so deeply moving as the death in childbirth of the girl
wife and the inarticulate grief and despair of the young
husband. The sobriety and clarity with which the scene is
presented make the pathos almost unendurable. I cannot
imagine why a writer with such genuine and profound compassion in him should be described as "cynical" and "cruel."
Or rather, I can imagine. People would like him to falsify his
clear-sighted vision of truth, and put false pathos into situations and characters Maugham rightly sees to be only deserv-
ing of ridicule and contempt.

But for a dramatist and fiction-writer it is not enough to
have a profound knowledge of people and the ability to
present them in words as they really are. There must be a
pattern of action. They must be showed, and showed con-
vincingly in action. We must see them entering a situation,
involved in it, and in the end admit freely that a life or lives
have been changed. Merely to suggest "atmosphere" and to
leave the reader to invent significance and imagine an ending
is evading the difficulty. The art of successful plotting may
seem an inferior one to those who have never attempted it.
Those who have made the attempt, know better. It is a
natural gift, which may be developed and perfected, but
cannot be acquired by mere industry. And the same is true of
the art de raconteur, which is not quite what is meant in
English by "telling a story." It is the art of telling a story in
such a manner that in spite of himself the reader or listener
is compelled to give his attention and interest. That, too, is a
natural gift.

All the "art and craft of fiction" theories about how these

two gifts may be acquired or simulated artificially are so much moonshine. Good stories, well told in print, well presented on the stage, are what the world is prepared to reward handsomely. If the art or knack of producing them could be taught or acquired, what a rush there would be! It is obvious from his early novels and plays that Maugham started with both the gift of narrative and the gift of plotting. It is also obvious that he has given much thought and pains to perfecting these gifts. In their fatuous way the critics have recognized this by dubbing Maugham "competent." The right word is "masterly." Maugham is one of those uncommon writers who think, and think clearly and thoroughly, before they begin to write. He never rambles or improvises. You feel that before he puts his pen to paper he is the master of all his characters and knows exactly what he intends to do with them. One result of all this is the uniformly high level of his writing, something of the unstrained excellence you find in the prose of Voltaire. If Maugham has good days and off days, there is no sign of it in his writing. When a story or a play seems better than some of the others, the only assignable reason is that somehow the intrinsic interest and excitement of the subject are greater. That is a purely personal matter for the reader, and perhaps explains why readers differ so much about what is "Maugham's best work."

One of the worst disadvantages of "the literary life" is its narrowness. Arthur Symons once said very truly that a villa and books never yet made a poet. And the kind of society generally frequented by literary people has seldom benefited a novelist. However unpleasant the experience may have been Maugham undoubtedly profited as a writer by contact with other kinds of life before literary success enabled him to live as he chose. And in later life it has been a distinct asset to him that he rather dislikes the company of literary people and is not a social star. His early stage successes forced him to meet well-known theatrical people and the pre-War social world of London. His work (*Theatre* for instance) shows that he made excellent use of the opportunity, but he refused to tie himself to fashionable social life. Most authors now travel extensively, but Maugham has the distinction of having travelled intelligently and observantly. What Spain has meant to him we know from *Don Fernando*. His wanderings in the Pacific and the Malay States and China have been made vivid for us in stories and plays. And the Ashenden series of works comes out of his experiences in the Secret Service during the War. All of it non-literary life.

Thus, Maugham's work gives the impression of coming from an accomplished man of the world and not from a man in a library. People enjoy this, and I believe it to be one of the secrets of his success. There is a double advantage. He has been able to make close observation of many types of person, usually ignored or despised by the littérateur. And, as I say, readers like his manner. It is so entirely free of any trace of condescension, pretentiousness and superciliousness —the besetting sins of the highbrow. It is not merely a question of good manners, but of an attitude to life which is far superior to the limited interests and prejudices of intellectualist cliques. Maugham is a pretty good bridge-player and does not hesitate to reveal the fact in his writings. If he had such an accomplishment, the average littérateur would not dare reveal it—unless of course Maugham's example has now made it fashionable. In a minor way this matter of bridge-playing is characteristic of Maugham's whole attitude to life and art. There has been a long process of shedding everything he thought factitious and not quite true to himself. He refuses to conform to anybody's idea of what he ought to think and feel and do, and has labored with the utmost sincerity to discover what he really does think and feel, what sort of things he really wishes to do. If he finds that he prefers to go to the South Seas rather than cash in socially on his success in London, he will go to the South Seas, however much the prevailing opinion may be that he "ought" to prefer dining out with the upper classes. If he finds he prefers Voltaire's prose to the prose of the Bible, he will say so, whatever the prevailing fashion. Out of such essential integrity and truth to himself comes the genuine artist.

Maugham has achieved popular and artistic success with plays, novels, and short stories. This is quite exceptional— think of Shaw's novels and Flaubert's plays. *The Gentleman in the Parlour, Don Fernando,* and *The Summing Up* are fascinating books of travel, reminiscence, anecdote, and criticism. *Don Fernando* is one of the pleasantest books on Spain I know, and conveys a great deal of knowledge about Spanish life, literature, history, and art with such ease and lightness of touch that a superficial reader might fail to see how much and how accurately he is instructed. *The Summing Up* contains admirable remarks on the art of writing, the more persuasive since they are presented with exquisite measure and modesty. It is a wonderfully varied record of fine achievements. What variety there is in his novels from *Of Human Bondage* with its tragic irony to the cordially acid wit of *Cakes and Ale;* in the stories from *Rain* and *The Downfall of Edward Barnard* to *The Alien Corn* and *The Hairless Mexican;* in the plays from *Our Betters* and *The Constant Wife* to the poignant tragedy of *For Service Rendered.* It is extraordinary that one man should write so much so well in such different genres.

I find pleasure in saluting Somerset Maugham, a master of the hard long art of writing, and I hope that more accomplished critics may be led to point out his achievements more adequately than I have been able to do.

5

Oscar Wilde

Almost everything that could possibly be said about Oscar Wilde has been said already ("tout a été dit"), including much that had better have been left unsaid. But, as is often the way with us human beings and our "points of view," this mass of printed material is more remarkable for diversity than for lucidity. The opinions of Wilde as human being run from the savage contempt of Mr. Justice Wills (sentencing him to virtual death) to the hero-worship of Sherard and Ross; and the estimates of his writings occupy many varying positions between the one extreme, that he was a ridiculous plagiarist and poseur, and the other extreme, that he was the greatest English (pardon! Irish) writer of the nineteenth century.

So far as I recollect, all the personal reminiscences of Wilde agree that his personality was more important than his talents, and his conversation more fascinating than his writings. This is not a hopeful thought for posterity which cannot have the privilege of listening to dear Oscar's talk which, according to Mr. E. F. Benson, was "like to the play of a sunlit fountain." Even Mr. G. B. Shaw, who writes about Wilde with prejudice (which is not surprising) and obtuseness (which is most surprising) admits the brilliance of Wilde's talk. But that is about as far as agreement goes, and seldom has the old tag about so many men, so many opinions been so fully justified as among the witnesses to Wilde's life and character.

At this date and distance we have always to keep in mind that for the contemporary world of newspaper readers Wilde

Introduction to *The Portable Oscar Wilde* (New York: The Viking Press, 1946).

began by being ridiculed as Bunthorne and ended up by being execrated as a kind of fatuously impudent would-be Nero who had sprawled full length in the gutter, where the amiable "world" took good care he should remain. So violent was the storm of "morality" against the unfortunate Wilde that only the most courageous dared at the time to say anything decent about him. So far as the "normal" men are concerned the attitude may be not too unfairly summarized as: "Of course, I never took Wilde really seriously, and for heaven's sake don't think I was that way myself, but he was *rather* amusing and some of his work isn't bad." Still, . . . these witnesses have contributed to the Wilde tradition, not to say legend.

The most voluminous memoirs of Wilde naturally come from those who to a greater or lesser extent shared his inter-sexual or bi-sexual nature. It is not surprising that they should try to make a hero of the man, a persecuted martyr, a genius wantonly destroyed by harried heterosexuals. If the evidence were no more complicated than that it would not be difficult to discount the heroics and to arrive at a coherent, if not perfectly accurate, idea of the man. What confounds the inquirer is the discovery that these fuglemen (as Harris rather aptly names them) could not remain loyal to their hero or refrain from insensate bickering among themselves, during the course of which they constantly change their ground and unsay what they have solemnly said. They could not refrain from joining in the bitterly useless debate of Oscar versus "Bosie." Which of the two was to blame for Oscar's downfall?—as if both had not behaved with insane folly and insolence!

To top this off the reader must know that the present text of *De Profundis* (the letter written by Wilde in Reading Gaol) is only part of the original, cleverly selected by Robert Ross to show Wilde in the best light possible. The suppressed portions of *De Profundis* (which I have read, but which apparently cannot be published until 1960) are not scandalous, but consist chiefly of a bitter review of Wilde's relations with Douglas up to and including the trial. From this (if Wilde is to be believed) it emerges that he was fascinated by Douglas and swayed by his influence, an influence which was disastrous. Douglas is shown as selfish and heartless, sponging on Wilde to pay for his extravagances, wasting Wilde's time, degrading him from an intellectual to a life of eating, drinking, and sloth. Finally Douglas, in his hatred of his father (he even threatened the life of Lord Queensberry) goaded Wilde into taking the legal action which resulted in his own conviction. "Bosie," in short, tried to put his father in prison and landed Oscar there instead.

The production of parts of the suppressed *De Profundis* in court lost Douglas a libel action he had brought against Arthur Ransome. This goaded him to one of the furies described by Wilde, and he produced a venomous diatribe called *Oscar Wilde and Myself*, which is so unbalanced that it disposes one to think that on the whole Wilde was telling the truth.

Still, this is not the whole extent of the confusion. Frank Harris appeared with *Oscar Wilde, his Life and Confessions*. Now, we all know about Frank Harris, a gifted and bumptious person who often lived by what he called "white-mailing," for whom Truth was something he had heard about, and who at the time he published this book privately in New York was a passionate pro-German and anxious to do anything to discredit the British. Of course, Harris had a right to his point of view about the War of 1914–18 (unfortunate as it turned out for him), but it can hardly be claimed as impartial. What is new in Harris's *Life* is seldom true, and the alleged *Confessions* do not sound authentic.

Many if not most of Wilde's letters seem to have been destroyed by the terrified recipients in 1895. Most of those which have been published relate to the post-prison epoch, but these have never been collected in one volume, and there are still others which have never been published.

When Arthur Ransome published his critical study in 1912 he wrote of "Wilde's vice." That was still the accepted view among men of letters, even those who admired Wilde's wit and writings, though it had long been abandoned by the pioneer psychologists of sex. Nothing better illustrates the change that has taken place in these matters in the past thirty years, the growing tolerance, than the fact that most writers would feel ridiculous if they used the word "vice." Unfortunately Science has not yet made up its mind on the subject. The biochemists and geneticists stress deficiency of hormones; the psychologists insist on early influences. May not both be partly right? Unlucky influences acting on a predisposed nature cause a deviation from what is somewhat smugly called the "norm," whatever that may be. At all events, public opinion nowadays would think the only too deplorably notorious "Wilde case" more a subject for psychiatrists and medical specialists than for English Criminal Law and the average stony English judge.

I am anxious to get away from this topic, but I brought it up in the beginning of this notice for two reasons. In the first place, if Wilde had not been a sort of martyr of homosexuality he would not have attained a fraction of his immense contemporary notoriety—hideous as the burden of it was to him in the wretched fag-end of life after Reading Gaol. (It is of course impossible to estimate what proportion of Wilde's reputation in the earlier half of the past half century was due to this fact and what was due to his literary talents, wit, and personality.) In the second place, the merest outline of Wilde's life is falsified unless we admit at once that he was always the homosexual type, always potentially liable to succumb to overt practices, though Ransome (I assume) had some private information leading him to fix the date so confidently at 1886.

It is a fact (which I suppose we can only deplore) that the male homosexual type often unconsciously annoys and irritates the average heterosexual male even when the latter (as frequently happens) is ignorant of what it is that annoys him. (The stupid popular word "sissie" indicates what I mean.) It was just this which made Wilde unpopular in spite of his wit and charm.

The traits in Wilde's character which were stressed to his detriment by his sexual make-up might be not unfairly described as affectation, vanity, folly, and a curious lack of judgment almost approximating a failure to correlate the actual world with his own private world of wish and fantasy.

I am not going to venture on so hazardous a piece of psychology as "the homosexual character" (for what then is "the heterosexual character"?) but I think these traits are often exaggerated in men of this type. In the origin they are probably harmless enough, but become envenomed by a hostile environment, which in turn reacts more violently, and so on until there is intense bitterness or a catastrophe. If we say of Wilde that he brought his fate on himself by inconceivable insolence and lack of judgment, what on earth are we to say of a society which behaved in the savage and unpardonable manner it did in 1895 and after? Nor was this confined to England, though England was the first culprit. As Vincent O'Sullivan (an Irishman) has pointed out, the most brutal attacks on Wilde came from America; and the moment the ex-convict landed in France he was warned by the sub-prefect that he would be instantly expelled if he caused any scandal.

In the height of his fame Wilde was usually referred to as "the brilliant Irishman." After 1895 he became the Anglais, the Englander, the Britisher. I note, *en passant*, that he has once more become the brilliant Irishman. "I have made my name a low byword among low people," he wrote of himself bitterly but truly. If he has been gradually redeemed from that degrading situation it is not because of the hero-worshipping or tales of "marvellous conversation" which has left practically no trace, but because of the merit of his writings and the general change in outlook.

Oscar Wilde was twenty when he went up to Oxford in 1874, and he already had a small but deserved reputation as a young classical scholar of promise. Indeed, his whole academic career was a series of successes, which could only have come from hard work and certain gifts which, as always in the young, might or might not develop into something notable. Wilde had already spent three years at Trinity College, Dublin, where he had been a Queen's Scholar and a University Scholar, and had come out high in classics Honors. He had taken a prize with an essay on the extant fragments of Greek Comic Dramatists. And he was a favorite pupil of Mahaffy, who acknowledged Wilde's assistance in the preface to his *Social Life in Greece*. It is perhaps necessary to explain to a generation which knows not Zion that Mahaffy lived to be provost of Trinity and president of the Royal Irish Academy, that he was the best classical scholar of his time in Ireland, and that several of his books on Greece remained in print for nearly half a century.

The "Greek sympathy," as Peacock charmingly calls the freemasonry of classical scholars, would naturally mean that the Magdalen dons watched the progress of the young Irishman discreetly but with interest. Would he keep up his intellectual life or would he waste his time in any of the half-hundred methods evolved by undergraduates to frustrate all efforts to educate them? Wilde's first answer to that was to win a "demyship" worth £95 a year for five years.

In those days Jowett was professor of Greek and Master of Balliol; Matthew Arnold had only recently ceased to lecture as professor of Poetry; Ruskin, as Slade professor, was exerting all his eloquence and knowledge of medieval art to civilize the young barbarians, though rapidly approaching the nervous and mental breakdown of 1878. These were powerful influences, but more delightful—because less official or entirely unofficial—were the English Romantic poets, the still living pre-Raphaelite poets and painters, that amusing and talented Mr. Whistler, and that retiring Brazenose don who had published some fascinating essays on the Italian Renaissance which Jowett had frowned upon— Walter Pater. All this was delightful to a sensitive, intelligent boy in the city of dreaming spires and old gray colleges and brilliant green lawns, with one of those pretty little brooks in England called a river. Moreover, chance had given Oscar Wilde the best undergraduate's rooms in Magdalen, which he furnished with blue china and engravings of female nudes, expressing the pious hope that he might live up to the blue china.

Of course, he was ragged by the hearties; he was an aesthete and a poet. It was said that at Oxford he read nothing but the English poets—if so, Mahaffy had grounded him wonderfully, for he took a First in Moderations, and then spent his vacation travelling with Mahaffy in Greece where he saw the German archaeologists recover the Hermes of Praxiteles. His Hellenic zeal made him late in coming up next term, and the dons fined him very heavily, but repentantly returned the money later when Wilde finished his Oxford career in a blaze of academic triumph, winning a First Class in Lit. Hum. and the Newdigate with his poem *Ravenna*.

When Oscar Wilde went down from Oxford for the last time, he had spent eight of his most impressionable years at universities. For good and for ill these years left their permanent mark on him. For one thing, his series of academic triumphs had made success necessary to him. In a world which is at best indifferent to and frequently hostile to the intellectual and aesthetic way of life, Wilde expected to be surrounded by admiring sympathizers; and as he was gifted with uncommon impudence and wit he made an enemy with every *mot*. He wanted life always to be as it had been at Oxford, when his father paid all the bills, when the university protected him from the world, and poured out for him the knowledge and beauty salvaged from the ages, and he was free to choose always what was lovely and refined and exquisite, and to reject all that was sordid and harsh and vile. He wanted to eat of all the fruits in the garden of life, he told a friend as they strolled along Magdalen Walk, but only those in the sunny side of the garden. He had taken too literally and was to apply too sensually, too coarsely, too selfishly Pater's wonderful words:

The service of philosophy, or speculative culture, towards the human spirit is to rouse, to startle it into sharp and eager observation. Every moment some form grows perfect in hand or face; some tone on the hills or the sea is choicer than the rest; some mood of passion or insight or intellectual excitement is irresistibly real and attractive for us—for that moment only. Not the fruit of experience, but experience itself, is the end. A counted number of pulses only is given to us of a variegated, dramatic life. How may we see in them all that is to be seen in them by the finest senses? How shall we pass most swiftly from point to point, and be present always at the focus where the greatest number of vital forces unite in their purest energy?

It was Wilde's error to want always to enjoy the ecstasy without paying the price beforehand in labor, in self-discipline, in restraint. He paid the price afterwards.

Yet when Oscar Wilde extravagantly took a first-class ticket from Oxford to London and treated himself to an armful of new books and periodicals to beguile that brief journey, he had already received warnings if he had not been too conceited to notice them. After a life of lavish expenditure Sir William Wilde had suddenly died, leaving only £7,000 to his wife and a small income to Oscar. The natural thing in such circumstances would have been for the Magdalen fellows to elect so brilliant a young graduate to a probationary fellowship, with the chance of a life income so long as he behaved himself and remained unmarried. The Magdalen dons ominously did nothing. With Wilde's academic record, this seems like a snub. Perhaps he had offended the dons; more likely, in their quiet way, they saw already the type he was and did not want him.

Young Wilde had "immeasurable ambitions"—at least, he thought he had. What he actually achieved when he had at last earned enough money to cut a figure in the great world, we shall see. He had been trained for no profession, and if he had been trained he would not have practiced successfully—like his fellow-countryman, Tom Moore, he was born a social entertainer and also within limits a writer. Indeed it is a mistake to rate Wilde too low as a writer. If he had not been a writer he would now be as nearly forgotten as those heroes of former scandals, Charles Parnell and Charles Dilke.

At this time Wilde had little enough to offer a publisher. He had his *Rise of Historical Criticism*, which would probably have won him another Oxford prize if the dons hadn't thought he had too many already. He had begun to write (with some unconscious prescience) a play about Russian revolutionaries. And he was completing a volume of poems.

For a good many years now it has been the custom to treat Wilde's poems with contempt—he was a plagiarist, a *précieux*, and he had not read Paul Éluard. Let it be remembered that much criticism of poetry is a long grinding of intellectual axes, a frightful competition for an almost non-existent market. Having nothing to sell in that line myself at the moment I hope I can speak with some detachment to those who disinterestedly care about poetry.

Of course Wilde's poems have faults. I even believe I could point out a few which have been overlooked by the most myopic censors. For example, in *The Burden of Itys,* which is a kind of expanded *Ode to a Nightingale* filled with aesthetic images, we suddenly trip over the prosaic eighteenth-century line: "The harmless rabbit gambols with its young . . ." Yet the poem is filled with beautiful suggestions and allusions, not all of which are native to the author. It must be remembered that Wilde came at the end of the last great period of poetry. Within less than a century there had been Blake, Burns, Wordsworth, Scott, Coleridge, Byron, Shelley, Keats, Tennyson, Browning, Arnold, Meredith, Rossetti, William Morris, Swinburne, and hosts of smaller people. It was impossible for so young a man, loving poetry as Wilde so clearly did, to write poems without reproducing what he had admired so intensely. When, in maturity, he wrote the *Ballad of Reading Gaol* out of the bitter intensity of his own experience, he was original enough.

In spite of their obvious debts to Milton, Keats, Tennyson, Rossetti, and Arnold (not to mention others), these early poems have considerable vitality and charm. You can take every one of them disapprovingly to pieces, yet they are readable in a way which more approved specimens of the art are not. They seem to make the Romantic poetry of England accessible to young readers who are not yet competent to appreciate the greater writers. They represent the moment when Romanticism became classical—corresponding to the Parnassians in France—but with a classicism of joyous reminiscence, not of plodding obedience to rule and precept. They should be taken in the spirit of the Latin poetry of the Renaissance, when the subtle flavors of innumerable older writers were enthusiastically enjoyed, when every line and phrase was drenched in older poetry, yet there was something new about it all, some final touch of the writer's own personality. What a real kinship there is between Wilde's methods and those of Poliziano in such a poem as that on violets:

Molles o violae, veneris munuscula nostrae,
    Dulce quibus tanti pignus amoris inest,
Quae vos quae genuit tellus? quo nectare odoras
    Sparserunt zephyri mollis et aura comas?

and Poliziano's exquisite Italian stanza which so clearly inspired Botticelli.

The most ambitious of Wilde's aesthetic poems are those
nominally on Hellenic themes (*The Garden of Eros, The
Burden of Itys, Charmides, Panthea, Humanitad*), and all
suffer from a curiously inaesthetic stanza, made of a quatrain
of alternately rhymed pentameters followed by a pentameter
rhyming with a "fourteener." It is clumsy, and the extra
syllables are nearly always either a *cheville* or force an
awkward run over to the next stanza. An amusing fact is that
this young man, who was soon to repudiate poor Nature with
such witty insolence, shows in these poems a considerable
knowledge and love of Nature—not indeed of the Greece
which is his theme but of the lush Thames Valley. His
observation was, however, not that of Wordsworth, still less
of Richard Jefferies; for instance, he makes the tench (a
bottom-feeding pond fish) "leap at the dragon-fly," an insect
no fish would attempt. Wilde's excessive love of flowers in
and out of his poems was often laughed at and probably still
is:

Soon will the musk carnation break and swell,
Soon shall we have gold-dusted snapdragon,
Sweet-William with his homely cottage-smell,
And stocks in fragrant blow;
Roses that down the alleys shine afar . . .

That, however, is not by Wilde, but by one of his Masters,
the austere Matthew Arnold.

Later—to finish with the Poems—after Wilde went to
France he took something from Gautier and the Verlaine of
Eaux-Fortes. The *Sphinx*, which some people prefer to his
other poems because it is unHellenic and unEnglish, comes
out of Flaubert's *Tentation de Saint Antoine* suggested by
the dialogue of the *Sphinx and the Chimaera*. Wilde may
have got other suggestions for this poem from Huysmans' *A*

Rebours (1884), but he knew French well enough to go direct to Flaubert, and indeed the technique of remote erudition made poetic is entirely Flaubertian. Wilde's last work in verse, *The Ballad*, is a repudiation of his whole artistic creed especially as regards poetry—it is contemporary, realistic, and sordid in theme, and contains philanthropic propaganda. The butterfly had certainly been broken on the treadmill.

Although in 1878–80 Wilde could show only a few scattered publications in periodicals, his personality was already attracting attention, and was extremely welcome to the satirists of *Punch* longing to curry favor with the middle classes by holding art up to ridicule. They had not had much success with such recluses and haters of newspaper notoriety as Burne-Jones, Rossetti, Morris, and Pater. (Tennyson had a horror and Arnold a genuine contempt for publicity.) But Wilde was what the satirists were looking for—a seemingly obvious charlatan. Gilbert's Bunthorne, which he had originally meant for Pater, was transferred hastily to Wilde.

Even before the newspapers got hold of him, the reputation made by Wilde's personality and aesthetic antics was far in excess of his achievements. It is said that an ardent female disciple holding forth was interrupted by a sweet old lady with: "But what has Mr. Wilde done, dear? Is he a soldier?" Perhaps the old lady wasn't such a fool as the indignant disciple thought. It is usually taken for granted that Wilde's silly aesthetic costume, his lilies and languors, his blue china ("them flymy little bits o'blue") and all the rest of it were taken from the hard-working, publicity-hating pre-Raphaelites. No doubt he stole his gilded rags from them, but his real master in the art of getting talked about was someone quite different, one of the most astute and attractive adventurers who ever worked himself from nothing to sway the fortunes of a great empire—Benjamin Disraeli.

Disraeli, like Wilde, had set out to conquer society by his wits and had done anything and everything to get himself talked about and to push his way—a Julien Sorel who blatantly succeeded. At the age of twenty-one Disraeli had written in an absurd novel of genius, "To enter into high

society a man must either have blood, a million, or genius."
Neither Disraeli nor Wilde had a million or "blood." It was
Disraeli who had strained every faculty to dominate the most
brilliant of his contemporaries by his *mots* and the brilliance
of his talk; and a group of them agreed that "the cleverest
fellow in the party was the young Jew in the green velvet
trousers." Moreover, young Dizzy made use of bad taste and
fancy dress to advertise himself, bursting upon the world in
"the black velvet dress-coat lined with white satin, the gorgeous gold flowers on a splendidly embroidered waistcoat,
the jewelled rings worn outside the white gloves, the evening
cane of ivory inlaid with gold and adorned with a tassel of
black silk."

Young Disraeli's real hero was not Brummel, as is igno-
rantly supposed, but Byron, who also in his day wore astonishing clothes and dazzled the world with his fame. And
Wilde, in turn, took Disraeli and Disraeli's novels as his
guide to worldly success with the English aristocracy. Just as
Dizzy dropped his dandyism like a hot potato when he began
to succeed in Parliament, so Wilde changed into the clothes
of a gentleman when he left America. But, in taking Disraeli
as a model, Wilde overlooked certain important factors. The
novels are exaggerated, they are caricatures of Disraeli's *arri-
visme*; moreover, the dandy antics and frantic *bons mots*
actually did him harm—lots of people still thought Disraeli a
mountebank until the magnificent speech introducing his
first budget; and then again, Wilde lacked much that Disraeli had—the concentrated ambition, the unflagging energy
and determination, the tireless patience and character of
granite. We know now what success was scored by master
and pupil, and can estimate their respective abilities in the
conduct of public life. It is odd that Wilde never noticed
Disraeli's remark—"the only way to keep him out of the
House of Correction was to get him into the House of
Commons."

Wilde's poems were published and went into several editions—of two hundred copies each. His sayings were re-
peated. He was constantly caricatured in *Punch*. But he
remained as poor and unimportant as ever. Nobody was

paying to see this puny Alcibiades cut the tail off the pre-Raphaelite movement. The real blot on Wilde's career as an artist is not Reading Gaol but the lecture tour in America. There is no particular turpitude in lecturing, even when the lecturer can be heard, and of course lecturing in America is much like lecturing anywhere else. Dickens made an immense success of his readings in America, but then Dickens had something of his own to offer which all English-speaking people were crazy to hear. Wilde had nothing of his own to give; he could only betray his masters by peddling them.

It has been said, but not proved, that Wilde was entrapped into making this tour by the impresario of Gilbert and Sullivan, who thought it necessary to show Americans just what was being parodied in Bunthorne. If true, the discredit falls not on Wilde, but on the perpetrators of a somewhat dirty deal. The turpitude of the thing lies in Wilde's willingness to degrade for the sake of a little money and a lot of cheap notoriety two generations of English poets, painters, and critics who had never lowered their flag to make money and who all hated cheap publicity. They had worked, as artists do work, silently and to put forth the best that was in them, living poorly when they were poor, mostly on small incomes and the purchases of a few patrons, disregarding the screams and squibs and "serious critics," and leaving the public to take or leave their work as it chose. After leaving it for a long time though with plenty of mud-throwing, the public had begun to take it. Furthermore, these writers and painters had never cared tuppence what other countries said about them—they left foreign denigration as unheeded and unanswered as the even more destructive "serious criticism" which is the most malicious form of impotence. And then Wilde made the whole thing ridiculous, opened the breach by which the attack of the Philistines could break in. Having done all the mischief possible, Mr. Wilde collected his few wretched dollars, dropped his mountebank's clothes into the Atlantic, and turned up disguised as an English gentleman in Paris where he started to try and clear himself by writing *The Sphinx*.

The money—and there was not much of it—derived from

American lectures was soon spent, and Wilde was back in London, generously giving help and shelter to a penniless poet, and himself earning a precarious income by lecturing in the provinces. In a moment of mental lassitude Wilde made the blunder (imagine Disraeli doing anything of equivalent folly!) of asking Whistler's help in composing a lecture on painting; for Whistler, at once the most generous and meanest of men, was certain to make public the obligation, to exaggerate it, and to twit his alleged friend without urbanity:

What has Oscar in common with Art? except that he dines at our tables and picks from our platters the plums for the pudding he peddles in the provinces. Oscar—the amiable, irresponsible, esurient Oscar.—(*The Gentle Art of Making Enemies*)

The most revealing item in that none too intelligent attempt at satire is the strange use of the word "amiable" as a term of abuse. It is true—Oscar *was* amiable, but who except the "Butterfly" would have thought of it as a demerit?

Poetry, posturing, and lecturing having all failed to conquer society, Wilde seems to have become desperate and plunged recklessly into reviewing and marriage. His wife was a sweetly pretty but stupid young woman with the significant attraction of a considerable dowry, which enabled the couple to set up at 16 Tite Street, Chelsea. This marriage, which inevitably could only turn out unhappily, took place on the 29th May, 1884, and there were two children. The problem of Wilde's ambiguous nature is certainly complicated by the fact that at an earlier time he had been in love (genuinely or as a pose?) with the beautiful Lily Langtry, while more than one personal friend at the time asserts that Mr. and Mrs. Wilde seemed very much in love and Oscar especially appeared very happy. It is not true to say that Wilde immediately accepted the editorship of the *Woman's World* to support his wife. He did not do that until June, 1887, after the birth of his two sons.

It was as a reviewer—in fact in the role of a journalist, which Wilde so foolishly affected to despise, that he began to find himself as a prose writer of workmanlike quality, though, it is true, he seldom again matched the grace and cadence of the end of *L'Envoi*, which was written in America. Considering that nearly all reviews are hastily written it is not surprising that so many are slovenly and dull, and hardly ever worth reprinting. Wilde's reviews stand up to this test amazingly well, especially those written for the freer atmosphere of the *Pall Mall Gazette*. Some of them are really witty, and only the long editorials for the *Woman's World* (Literary and Other Notes) are so toned down to their audience as to be insipid. Quite a number of afterwards famous *mots* and passages for *Intentions* first appeared in these *Pall Mall Gazette* reviews.

It was an ironic twist of circumstances which for two years compelled Wilde, as editor of the *Woman's World*, to write flattering chronicles of a sex in which he daily became less interested. But the eighties were the period of Wilde's development and of his real work. Though still bitterly pursued by *Punch* (which having once found a joke is reluctant to drop it in case of never hitting on another) Oscar Wilde was socially successful, and was welcomed at many a luncheon and dinner table for the pleasure guests took in his talk. He visited Paris, not now as an unknown aesthete retreating from America with ignominy, but as a social figure to be written up in the French press by his friend, Robert Sherard. He met Moréas and Verlaine, Mallarmé, Gourmont, and Gide—perhaps also Huysmans, whom he greatly admired. I do not know what Yeats means by saying that Wilde talked "with a manner and music that he had learnt from Pater *or Flaubert*," for though Wilde certainly "fluted" like Pater he never met Flaubert (who moreover died in 1880), and if he had tried any of his aesthetic blarney on the sage of Croisset would have received as ferocious a snub as Henry James when he made the monstrous remark in Flaubert's presence that the Duc de Saint-Simon is a bad writer. From this distance it looks as if Wilde's Paris acquaintances were chiefly among the upper Bohemia—the kind of people who are aristocrats to artists, or artists to aristocrats.

With his customary good nature Wilde never complained of the hack-work he had to do for the *Woman's World* (the only writing of his which is virtually lifeless and uninteresting) or of his reviewing, which he rather enjoyed within limits. But work is a habit like everything else, and it was during the last half of the eighties that Wilde did much of the work which brought him genuine fame in the nineties. Once more he looked about for some form of literary activity which would enable him to express the charm of his personality, to employ effectively his talents and accomplishments. He now in quick succession tried the fairy tale, the short story, the Platonic dialogue, and the novel. In every one of these he obtained brilliant results, except perhaps in the short story when it was not a parable or prose poem.

The publication in book form of *The Happy Prince and Other Tales* in 1888 brought a letter of commendation from Walter Pater, and at last furnished an answer to catty old ladies who wanted to know what Mr. Wilde had *done*, and was he a soldier? "The Canterville Ghost"—somewhat too obviously aimed at the American public—was published in a periodical in 1887. Two years later "Pen, Pencil and Poison," "The Portrait of Mr. W. H.," and "The Decay of Lying" were issued serially. We can see how anxiously Wilde was looking for a form to please a wide public from the diversity of his attempts at this time. "The Sphinx Without a Secret" and the "Model Millionaire" are simply magazine stories and better passed over in silence. "The Canterville Ghost" is better, an attempt at supernatural farce—a somewhat distant tribute to Edgar Poe. "Pen, Pencil and Poison," is a biographical sketch of Wainewright, author and aesthete, forger and perhaps poisoner. Egotists seldom make good biographers, tending as they must do to exhibit themselves rather than their nominal subjects; so the chief interest of this study is extraneous, the melancholy coincidence that Wainewright too was a man of culture and talents who stood his trial, and was sentenced to transportation for life.

"The Portrait of Mr. W. H." is more original, ingenious, and entertaining, for, by a clever manipulation of extracts from Shakespeare's *Sonnets* Wilde makes out a seemingly excellent case for believing that the sonnets were written to a Mr. W. H., or Willie Hughes, a handsome boy actor who supposedly played women's parts on the Elizabethan stage.

Apart from the serious obstacle that no such person as Willie Hughes is known to have existed, a study of the sonnets alongside Wilde's fictionalized essay shows at once how he has solicited the text. Still, the idea so much fascinated him, that he persuaded Ricketts to paint him, in the style of Clouet, a portrait of Mr. W. H. It was not very wise to write this essay, and in the state of public opinion at that day publication was madness. Apart from other dangerous implications, there is particular emphasis on the cult of "Alexis" by certain minor Elizabethan poets; and as everyone knows "Alexis" names the second eclogue of Virgil, "Formosum pastor Corydon ardebat Alexin, Delicias domini" . . . a beautiful poem but flagrantly homosexual. To anyone who had read Virgil—and at that time most upper class Englishman had—"The Portrait of Mr. W. H." was an unequivocal declaration and an insolent defiance. Prudent men began to drop Mr. Wilde.

Nevertheless, so pleasant and charming was Wilde in company that many people—in spite of evidence which now looks so obvious—refused to believe anything against him. The late Wilfrid Scawen Blunt used to give an annual dinner at Crabbet Park to a small group of distinguished friends he called the Crabbet Club—members were automatically expelled when they became prime ministers or pro-consuls. It was the custom that each new member should be charged after dinner with any and all misdoings charged to him by public gossip, and against this he had to defend himself. Well, I once spent a week-end with Mr. Blunt, and he told me that when Wilde was the new member of the club he was attacked rather savagely by George Wyndham (an uncle of Lord Alfred Douglas, who was also related to Blunt) and that Wilde got up and made so witty and laughable a speech, humorously admitting everything of which he was afterwards convicted but excusing it all on the ground of its being necessary to his art that Mr. Blunt at any rate was wholly convinced of his innocence. (Douglas gives a very different version of this episode; I relate it as nearly as I can remember Mr. Blunt telling it.) People apparently thought that homosexuality was a mere affectation with

Wilde, like sunflowers and allegedly aesthetic clothes. These had been discarded for conventional garb, so very likely when the full advertising value had been derived from this other very dangerous "pose" Mr. Wilde would subside into respectability with a bevy of chorus girls.

Wilde really found himself as a writer and easily excelled all he had hitherto published with "The Decay of Lying" which was followed in 1890 by two even better Platonic dialogues which appeared in *The Nineteenth Century*, while *The Picture of Dorian Gray* was coming out serially in *Lippincott's Magazine*. The form of the dialogue has often been used by English writers who hoped to give a light tone to reflections and ideas, from Dryden's *Of Dramatic Poesy* and Bishop Berkeley's *Three Dialogues between Hylas and Philonous in Opposition to Sceptics and Atheists* to Flecker's *The Grecians* and Sturge Moore's *Hark to These Three Talk about Art*; but none has produced dialogues so readable, so witty, so colored, so eloquent and—in spite of the sneerers—so solidly constructed and full of thought and good sense.

Certainly, in these dialogues there are faults of affectation, of paradox not more than half true, of exuberance—but surely we may forgive the paradoxes for their wit, the exuberances for their beauty, and even the affectations for their harmlessness. "The Decay of Lying" was a plea for imagination and the *beau idéal* as against the then rising school of realists, unfortunately still with us, who "find life crude and leave it raw." Pater, breathing the serene air of Oxford, held that "all art aspires to the condition of music"; but Wilde seems to have had a momentary prescience of the horror that was coming, when all art would aspire to the condition of journalism.

I shall not dwell upon the wide reading of these three dialogues, reading which is used lightly and appreciatively, to give the reader pleasure, to stimulate appreciation, to communicate enthusiasm. It is one of the many misfortunes of our times that under the stress of our apparently infinite public calamities we are forgetting how to admire, that we who have much to learn from our predecessors in the arts think it becoming to treat them with the full contempt of ignorance. Like his masters in criticism, Ruskin, Pater, and J.

A. Symonds, Wilde believed that criticism exists to help people to enjoy art, not to disgust them by wearisome superiorities and a kind of aesthetic browbeating.

For a detailed and sympathetically intelligent analysis of *Intentions* I refer the reader to pages 104–29 of Arthur Ransome's *Oscar Wilde*. Mr. Ransome seems to have hit off the secret of this book's continued vitality and charm in the sentence where he speaks of "the fresh and debonair personality that keeps the book alive, tossing thoughts like roses, and playing with them in happiness of heart."

In his unaccountable endorsement of Frank Harris's work on Wilde, Mr. Bernard Shaw makes the astonishing statement that Wilde knew nothing about music or painting, while he (Mr. Shaw) had listened to his family practicing concertos for public performance and had studied the pictures at the Dublin Art Gallery. Now, Wilde never claimed to be a critic of music, and only refers to musicians *en passant*; and it is a notorious fact that many poets are quite unappreciative of music. Wilde has been sneered at for speaking (affectedly, it is true) of Dvořák's "mad scarlet thing," as if he imagined Dvořák was a painter; but Wilde was probably thinking of Rimbaud's sonnet on the color of sounds and the elaborate (not to say ridiculous) color theories of René Ghil.

Chesterton and Mr. Shaw are Wilde's two most distinguished imitators, taking up the manner of his paradox and using it for propaganda purposes—the one for catholicism, the other for communism. Mr. Shaw is among the greatest pamphleteers in English and has written admirable talkies for the stage, but he is mistaken about Wilde's knowledge of painting. It is true that only a dozen or fifteen painters are mentioned in *Intentions* and those rather obvious ones, but from Wilde's more fugitive writings (which Mr. Shaw doubtless overlooked) I have collected references to thirty-two painters, including such precise recollections as Guido's *Saint Sebastian in Genoa*, Perugino's *Ganymede in Perugia*, Correggio's *Lily-bearer in the Cathedral at Parma*, and so on. Wilde may of course have taken these references from Symonds or Ruskin (whose first-hand knowledge of medieval and renaissance painting respectively has rarely been equalled), but it looks as if they were genuine. At any rate Wilde cites painters so diverse as Angelico and Boucher, Blake and Giorgione, Mantegna and van Huysum. I am not claiming that he was a "critic" of painting, such as the erudite Crowe and Cavalcaselle, or the purist Bernard Berenson, or the very German Maier-Graefer. All I claim is that Wilde had indisputably seen more pictures than those in the Dublin Art Gallery, and cared about them as a source of artistic pleasure.

Wilde's latent dramatic talent must surely be counted among the reasons for the success of his dialogues. Wilde had always loved the stage, and before 1890 had made more than one unsuccessful attempt at tragedy. Now that he was "getting warm," as children say, and coming nearer his vocation of comedy, he was temporarily diverted by Lippincott's offer for him to write a novel, which resulted in *The Picture of Dorian Gray*. One of the most striking facts about this book has nothing whatever to do with its merits or demerits as a novel. It is that the character of Dorian Gray and his relationship to Lord Henry Wotton (Wilde) were imagined and written down before Wilde had met Lord Alfred Douglas. The subsequent reality seemed to give substance to the paradox about Life imitating Art; and when Robert Hichens published *The Green Carnation* from a study of Wilde and Douglas in Egypt he often seemed to be parodying the conversations in *The Picture of Dorian Gray*. Take this, for instance:

"Oh! he has not changed," said Mr. Amarinth [Wilde]. "That is so wonderful. He never develops at all. He alone understands the beauty of rigidity, the exquisite serenity of the statuesque nature. Men always fall into the absurdity of endeavouring to develop the mind, to push it violently forward in this direction or in that. The mind should be receptive, a harp waiting to catch the winds, a pool ready to be ruffled, not a bustling busybody, for ever trotting about on the pavement looking for a new bun shop."

The parody is so close to imitation that it only gives itself away at the end of the last sentence. *The Green Carnation* is in fact so much like Wilde that it is the best thing Hichens ever wrote.

The Picture of Dorian Gray is a literary man's novel, an exposition of Wilde's hedonism, and, like all his writing, so dominated by the author's personality that all other characters are reduced to shadows. Several books have been suggested as the basis of this novel—Balzac's *La Peau de Chagrin* (1831), J. K. Huysmans' *A Rebours* (1884), R. L. Stevenson's *The Strange Case of Dr. Jekyll and Mr. Hyde* (1886). I see a little of Balzac's novel and a good deal of Stevenson's in *Dorian Gray*. But when people go so far as to hint that the whole novel was lifted from Huysmans, I can hardly believe that they can have read *A Rebours*. It is true that *A Rebours* is the French novel which "fascinated" Dorian Gray, and that its hero Des Esseintes is an aesthete who delights in the "perverse" and "artificial." Beyond that the resemblance ceases. Wilde's chapter on jewels can hardly be derived from *A Rebours* (which hasn't much about precious stones except for the episode of the tortoise encased in gold and gems), and the chapter on tapestry and embroidery comes from Ernest Lefébvre's *Embroidery and Lace*, the English translation of which Wilde had reviewed. Des Esseintes is a misanthropic, dyspeptic, prematurely impotent, neurotic Parisian who retires from Paris to complete isolation, sleeping by day and getting up by night, occasionally enlivened by some ghastly sexual nightmare, and trying to whip up his senses by such witty devices as collecting flowers which look as if they were made of zinc, pondering the last sterile drippings of the imitators of the generation of 1830, reading Latin poets of the Dark Ages (taken by Huysmans not from the originals but from Ebert's *Allgemeine Geschichte der Literatur des Mittelalters*), taking an imaginary trip to England by smelling a tarry rope, reading Dickens and Baedeker and drinking port in a bodega, and the like. The intense *taedium vitae* which drove Huysmans eventually to the Church finds full expression in this work. But what a contrast to *The Picture of Dorian Gray*! In comparison the bloom of health is on its cheek. Wilde's fault was not a sterile *taedium vitae* but "too much love of living"; and few more amiably sociable men ever lived. Wilde's book is full of amusing if affected talk and witticisms; whereas Des Esseintes rarely gets beyond such refined eloquence as " 'Sapristi!' fit-il enthousiasmé." A *Rebours* is all sulky monologue and self-pity, where *Dorian Gray* for all its affected sins and tragical ending is full of enjoyment and sunny talk. *The Picture of Dorian Gray* owes little to A *Rebours*; but on the other hand *Salome* owes a good deal.

Perhaps the weakest scenes in *Dorian Gray* occur in Chapters 17 and 18, when Wilde was growing weary of his imposed task and tried to brighten things up a bit with a snappy Duchess. Unluckily indeed, instead of making her talk like Wilde he tried to make her talk like the characters in a Meredith novel—and the result is dreadful, though it proves a misplaced reverence for the author of *The Egoist*. But to find the real origin of the "magic picture" idea which is, after all, the central part of the novel's plot, just as the talk and "philosophy" are its real excuse, we must go back to a book which appeared in 1826.

Wilde christened his first novel *Dorian Gray* and his second son Vivian; and Benjamin Disraeli called his first novel, *Vivian Grey*. This book is a remarkable though most unequal performance, full of insolence and naïveté, with some excellent thumb-nail sketches of character and a heap of epigrams wasted in a frantic purposeless plot and floods of would-be German romanticism. Far more than Browning's style it deserves Wilde's phrase "chaos illuminated by flashes of lightning." I suppose (though I don't know) that Wilde read this book as a boy in his mother's library, and found in it the theme of *The Picture of Dorian Gray*, as he had found hints and inspiration for his career in the life and works of Disraeli. Since to the best of my knowledge this has never been pointed out before I may perhaps be forgiven for quoting this curious piece of Disraeli juvenilia:

Max Rodenstein was the glory of his house. A being so beautiful in body and in soul you cannot imagine, and I will not attempt to describe . . . The only wish of Baroness Rodenstein, which never could be accomplished, was the possession of a portrait of her youngest son, for no consideration could induce Max to allow his likeness to be taken. His old nurse had always told him that the moment his portrait was taken he would die. The condition upon which such a beautiful thing was allowed to remain in the world was, she always said, that his beauty should not be imitated. About three months before the battle of Leipsic, Max was absent at the University, which was nearly four hundred miles from Rodenstein Castle, there arrived one morning a large case directed to the Baroness. On opening it it was found to contain a picture, the portrait of her son. The colouring was so vivid, the general execution so miraculous, that for some moments they forgot to wonder at the incident in their admiration of the work of art. In one corner of the picture, in small characters yet fresh, was an inscription which on examining they found consisted of these words: "Painted last night. Now, lady, thou hast thy wish." My aunt sank into the Baron's arms. . . .

The next day they received letters from Max. He was quite well, but mentioned nothing of the mysterious painting.

Three months afterwards, as a lady was sitting alone in the Baroness's room, and gazing on the portrait of him she loved right dearly, she suddenly started from her seat, and would have shrieked, had not an indefinable sensation prevented her. The eyes of the portrait moved. The lady stood leaning on a chair, pale and trembling like an aspen, but gazing steadfastly on the animated portrait. It was no illusion of a heated fancy; again the eyelids trembled there was a melancholy smile, and then they closed. The clock of Rodenstein Castle struck three . . . Three days afterwards came the news of the battle of Leipsic and at the very moment that the eyes of the portrait closed Max Rodenstein had been pierced by a Polish Lancer!

A little further on, apropos other things, is the sentence: "I fancy that in this mysterious foreigner, I have met a kind of double of myself"; and a page or two beyond Disraeli speaks of "an intellectual Don Juan, reckless of human minds, as he was of human bodies, a spiritual libertine." Put these together with Dr. Jekyll and Mr. Hyde, and you have the basis for *The Picture of Dorian Gray*. Of course Disraeli probably picked up his idea from the German Romantics, but the interesting thing is Wilde's skill in bringing up to date and breathing life into this obsolete fustian.

At this point I should like to pause a moment and to ask the reader to consider more particularly Wilde's method of building a piece of writing. Absolute originality in art is a delusion. Not only are we all the sons of somebody in any art, but the "higher" our aims the greater the number of predecessors to whom we are indebted. Willed originality is false originality. The only true originality is unconscious or at least unplotted—a spontaneously fresh way of looking at the world, a new personality. All writers borrow from others, consciously or unconsciously. The successful—I mean artistically successful—do it consciously, and justify themselves by claiming they have improved their thefts. Writers who try to avoid these obligations and labor to appear original are inevitably either dull or absurd. Such is Wilde's implied line of argument.

As a poet, as a critic, as a novelist, and as a dramatist, Wilde openly takes material from many sources and puts them together in the confident belief that he is making a new synthesis, that his unique personality will transform his borrowings. I have touched on a few of the sources of Wilde's poems, dialogues and *The Picture of Dorian Gray*; and the reader's degree of esteem for Wilde as a writer will, to some extent, depend on how far he thinks Wilde did succeed in remaking these borrowings into something fascinating and new. Those who accuse Wilde of plagiarism are in a sense right, but the borrowing is too open for it to be considered as anything but a deliberate plan. For instance, in the very first paragraph of "The Decay of Lying" there is a sentence about the mist on the hills looking like the bloom on a ripe plum; and this was taken from a contemporary poet whose work Wilde had reviewed, picking out this very image for praise and quotation. A little further on he amusingly picks up Whistler's phrase about "having the courage of the opinions of others" (a phrase Whistler had used of course against Wilde), and appropriates it without any acknowledgement. To those who are doubtful, I would say: "Very well, show me art criticism which has the quality and wit of Wilde's dialogues, bring me another novel like *Dorian Gray*, or even poems with that 'something' Wilde added to his poetic borrowings."

Returning for a moment to *The Picture of Dorian Gray*— it seems reasonable to suppose that Wilde did not care very much about this supernatural portrait idea he had borrowed from Disraeli's forgotten first novel. It pleased the commercial publisher, helped to create the effect of an aesthetic novel, provided a facile "moral" (for which Wilde did not care tuppence, but which the public then demanded), and provided—so to speak—a rough framework of sticks on which the modeller could build his group.

Actually there is only one character in the book—Oscar Wilde. The notion of dual personality was evidently in vogue at the time, as shown by the enormous success of *Dr. Jekyll and Mr. Hyde*. Wilde had a genuine case to display in himself. Lord Henry Wotton is Wilde as he hoped to remain, Dorian Gray as he feared he would become. It almost seems as if Wilde were warning himself throughout the book that as long as he kept his theories (i.e., his homosexuality) to the realm of pure Platonism and idealistic art, he was safe; but that as soon as he transferred them to the sphere of action he was courting disaster. Many of his contemporaries noted, with surprise, the vein of shrewd common sense in Wilde. It comes out in Henry Wotton when Dorian Gray hints to him that he has murdered Basil Hallward—Lord Henry shrugs it off and says, "My dear fellow, one should never do anything one can't talk about after dinner."

The novel then is an attempted projection into life of Pater's phrase about "the dialogue of the soul with itself." What conclusion Wilde actually came to is hard to say, for he was constricted on all sides by prejudices and commercial obligations, so that the end of the book is both melodramatic and dull. Perhaps its real ending comes when Dorian decides to renounce Hetty, and finds he has only added hypocrisy to his other crimes. A man cannot escape the consequences of his temperament, Wilde implies; even when he tries to do the conventional "right thing" he merely blunders. And then, after all, what is it the "world" punishes? Not crime, but the error of being found out; not squalid meanness, cheating, oppression, and humbug, but distinction, beauty, genius, culture, all that is above the average:

There is a fatality about all physical and intellectual distinction, the sort of fatality that seems to dog through history the faltering steps of kings. It is better not to be different from one's fellows. The ugly and the stupid have the best of it in this world. They can sit at their ease and gape at the play.

How true that is! It is not the whole tragedy of Man, but it is one of his tragedies. And how odd it seems that Wilde, knowing all this, should have acted as he did, that even as he wrote these paragraphs of wordly—and world—wisdom, he was digging the grave of his own career and all he cared for with frenzied folly. He was on the verge of that financial success which was to add *hybris* to his other errors—*hybris,* that insolent excess against which his masters of the Greek drama and Greek philosophy had warned him. At the same time he met in the person of Alfred Douglas that pinchbeck Antinous with whom he was to play the part of a fatuous and feeble Hadrian.

Wilde had for years been trying to write a successful play. In 1883 he returned to America in the hope that V*era* might be produced, and the *Duchess of Padua* actually was produced in 1891 at the Broadway Theatre, New York. But his first success was with *Lady Windermere's Fan* (20th February, 1892) in London; shortly after which a license was refused for *Salome*. The earlier and minor plays may be safely neglected, which reduces those to be considered to three comedy-dramas, one comedy-farce, and a tragedy. By general consent *Salome* and *The Importance of Being Earnest* are placed at the head of Wilde's stage writings; and for once general consent is quite right, though the other three are by no means wholly the negligible imitations they are supposed to be.

Wilde had two distinct styles of writing, though he sometimes mixed them (as in the dialogues) with the happiest results. One of these was the aesthetic or symbolist, gorgeous and poetic, full of allusion and reminiscence and jewelled words (the purple patch, as it is aptly called), and the other light, worldly, cynical, paradoxical, full of laughter. In his plays he nearly always kept them apart, and on the few occasions when he does attempt the purple patch in his comedy-dramas, the result is failure. It was grotesque to make drawing-room characters suddenly talk the speech of *Salammbô* and the *Tentation*; but it was absolutely appropriate for Salome.

The tale of Salome dancing before the tetrarch Herod, and

demanding as her reward "the head of John the Baptist on a charger" is a world story, and belongs to any artist or writer who thinks himself strong enough to re-handle it. It appears first, at no more than anecdote length, in the 14th chapter of the Gospel of St. Matthew and the 6th of St. Mark. The name "Salome" is not mentioned in the Gospels, but she is the "daughter of Herodias." The theme was often handled by the old masters. Rubens painted a Salome, and a picture of her by a Venetian master used to hang in the National Gallery; and there are many others.

The theme came up again in France in the late seventies and early eighties. Gustave Moreau, a painter who could not rest content with "visual experiences" of two oranges and a banana, produced a number of detailed visions of imaginary scenes between 1850 and his death. He painted two pictures of the Salome legend, one before the dance, and the other, *L'Apparition*, showing with great power and the most gorgeous decorative ensemble Salome's hallucinated vision of the decapitated saint after she has earned her reward. The picture was one of the most discussed at the Salon of 1876.

Did Flaubert see these pictures? I think he probably did and they suggested his story of Herodias—first mentioned in his correspondence, apparently as a new idea for a story, in an undated letter to Madame des Genettes, placed by Madame Commanville in May 1876—the month of the spring salon. On this story Flaubert concentrated his erudition, his personal knowledge of the Neart East, and the limitless resources of his meticulous prose style. He developed the story far beyond the cursory summary of the New Testament, created and motivated the characters, constructed the setting, and made the seemingly purposeless murder credible. As often with Flaubert, the end is severely toned down and matter of fact. The disciples flee with John's head—"As it was very heavy they carried it alternately."

Then came Huysmans with the *A Rebours* we have already dipped into apropos *The Picture of Dorian Gray*. Several over-written pages are there devoted to an interesting interpretation of Moreau's pictures and, as the critics put it, "a note of perversity and sadism is added." This was in 1884,

and not long afterwards Wilde began talking about a play on
Salome, telling people his version of it, and constantly
changing his mind about the treatment of Salome's character. "Plagiarism!" But whose? Wilde had as much right to
make use of the work of his predecessors as Huysmans, as
much right to dramatize Flaubert, Moreau, and Huysmans
as Shakespeare himself had to take a play from a new novel
by Robert Greene or a short story by Giraldi Cinthio or the
legends of Hollingshead. As to Wilde's having taken the
method from Maeterlinck, it seems from what Sherard says
that he must have been at work on it before Maeterlinck's
first play was published.

Wilde has been successful in reconstituting this grotesque
old tragedy, and in supplying dramatic motivations avoided
by his predecessors. Flaubert kept close to the ancient narrative, and made Salome the tool of her mother Herodias,
while he supplied the description of the famous dance from
his recollections of the performance given by an Arab harlot
he met in Egypt. Wilde, on the other hand, brings Salome
into the foreground at once, and keeps her there. He takes
up Huysmans's hint of the predatory lust of Woman, and
makes Salome fall in love with the chaste saint who of
course rebuffs her with a good deal of scriptural insult.
Seeing her stepfather, the tetrarch, is obviously hankering
after her, Salome dances for him against the strenuous opposition of her mother, after having made him promise a reward "even to half my kingdom." The end is startlingly dramatic. As Salome in a frenzy of remorse and sinister blood-
lust kisses the lips of the severed head, Herod in a spasm of
jealousy and remorse, orders his soldiers: "Kill that woman!"

Here again we see Wilde's habitual method of openly
taking material from sources everyone knew and recombining
them into something original, coloring and dominating them
by his personality. I incline to believe him when he says that
he used the repetitions in Salome (which Max Nordau in his
Degeneration solemnly proclaimed to be an infallible sign of
cretinism!)—that he used these repetitions to give the effect
of the refrain in an old ballad. This would give him priority
over Maeterlinck—not that it matters, but after all Wilde

was writing Symbolist poems years before the Symbolist movement began. He was certainly aided in writing the French by Pierre Louÿs and Marcel Schwob, but their help did not go beyond making verbal corrections. Writing the play in French has been censured as an affectation, as if half the poets of England from Chaucer and Gower to Swinburne have not written in other languages! The practice has only disappeared with the vogue of the uneducated author. Besides, there were sound artistic reasons for writing *Salome* in French. Effects are possible with French which cannot be obtained by English; and then the Salome legend Wilde treated was so largely the creation of French artists that it was not only a proper homage to them to write the play in French, but the whole feeling and atmosphere of the story demanded it. Anyway, the play as it stands is much better in French than in Douglas's translation, although that was revised and corrected by Wilde.

I am at a disadvantage in discussing the three comedy-dramas, which, the dramatic critics tell us, are the characteristic Wilde re-working of known material—in this case the plays of Augier and Dumas *fils*, with elements from Scribe and Sardou. I have long felt that life is both too short and too pleasant to spend any of it in reading the boulevard plays of the Second Empire. However, anyone who has been to the theater will recognize in these plays stock situations, stock characters, stock morals, and stock accessories—in fact, that stock view of life which for some quaint reason is known as "realism" in the theater. There are the wronged woman and the wicked lord, the good woman who seems to trip and the bad woman who saves her, the successful politician with a skeleton in his bank account and the female blackmailer from Vienna, the compromising letter, the all-important fan, bracelet, glove, *tirade à faire, nous aurons des larmes, et caetera, et caetera* . . . What is original in these three pieces is the dominating Wilde personality. Except when they are being moral to please the stalls or dramatic to please the gallery, all the characters talk like Oscar Wilde; and it is this amusing talk with its mixture of nonsense, affectation, and shrewd wisdom which has kept these plays from oblivion.

A *Woman of No Importance* is the worst of the three. The fact that the first act consists almost entirely of talk is not unwelcome to a reader, though the audience (one surmises) must have fidgeted a good deal. Is this witty froth meant to warn the discerning that Mr. Wilde is plotting with his tongue in his cheek? At any rate, he must have known that in real life his penny tract morality would have been completely disregarded. After twenty years of poverty the wronged woman would have been only too delighted to see her "nameless boy" rescued from a bank clerk's stool to become private secretary to his illegitimate father, now wealthy, powerful, and feared as Lord Illingworth. She herself would have jumped at the chance of marrying Illingworth, even though it was only a marriage in name—for it would have given her wealth, position, leisure, and the frequent company of her son in his new career. As to the Puritan maiden (fished out of *The Courtship of Miles Standish*, one surmises) who denounces Society as a leper smeared with gold, she is a grotesque, a parody of self-righteous cant. However, the theater audiences swallowed it all and applauded—this was what they had been taught to believe and what they came to hear. The one sensible person in the play, who says any number of good things, is the villain, Lord Illingworth, who was probably hissed and catcalled by the boxes as he left the stage for his dressing-room, to remove his wig and grease paint and reveal the smiling features of Mr. Oscar Wilde.

Lady Windermere's Fan and *An Ideal Husband* are better. Lady Windermere is an aggressively chaste woman who has a disreputable mother without knowing it—they must have been giants for keeping secrets in those days. The mother turns up as Mrs. Erlynn (from Vienna? I believe so), and Lord Windermere foolishly gives her money and tries even to arrange a social comeback without telling his wife anything about it. (In fact the real moral of the play is: Never do a silly thing without first telling your wife.) Lady Windermere naturally suspects her husband of a love affair with Mrs. Erlynn, and as an intelligent contribution to the situation compromises herself (the fan!) with Lord Darlington, from which she is nobly saved—you've guessed it! by her unknown mother. In doing so Mrs. Erlynn has hopelessly compromised herself, thereby of course confirming everybody's worst suspicions; but the author is merciful and lets her marry her Tubby (Lord Augustus Something-or-other) who, curiously enough, talks like the Scarlet Pimpernel years before that superman was invented.

An Ideal Husband is perhaps a little more emancipated, but . . . It is the blackmail play. Sir Robert Chiltern, a successful politician on the verge of cabinet rank, has a Secret in his life. Mrs. Cheveley (did I mention that she was from Vienna?) attempts to profit by it in no uncertain terms, but is happily defeated by a bracelet and Lord Goring.

On the whole it may be said that the moral of these three dramas is that really "good" women cause a great deal more trouble than they are worth; though of course such was not the intention of the author (at least, explicitly) nor the understanding of his delighted audience. *The Importance of Being Earnest* is a very happy transfer of literary allegiance from the fustily moral dramatic school of nineteenth-century France to the happier days of Wycherley and Congreve. *The Importance of Being Earnest* is a comedy-farce without a moral, and it is a masterpiece. Mr. Bernard Shaw (for one astounding moment appearing in the guise of Mrs. Grundy) denounces it as a "thoroughly heartless play" (in which he is supported by that unspotted Galahad, Frank Harris), which is sheer nonsense. *The Importance of Being Earnest* is not heartless, it is delightfully and amusingly light-hearted. For a masterly stroke of visual comedy there is nothing better than the appearance of Jack Worthing in deepest mourning for the death of his fictitious brother, Earnest, when the audience knows that Algy Moncrieff masquerading successfully as that brother is having a delightful meal inside the house with pretty Cecily Cardew. This grotesque figure of gloom among the roses and the sunshine is no bad figure of Victorian morality, and it was very nice of Wilde to make the Victorians laugh at it.

With three artistically immoral plays and one masterpiece Wilde had achieved the money he thought he needed to realize his "immeasurable ambition," for which he had worked perhaps harder than is usually supposed. His income in the nineties is said to have been about £8,000 a year. These were gold pounds in a day when income tax was negligible and goods and services much cheaper. Goodness knows what astronomical figure in supertaxed paper pounds a man would have to earn now to enjoy their real equivalent. But when Wilde had at last got his opportunity, what did his "immeasurable ambition" lead him to achieve? The post of Prime Minister, like his unacknowledged master Disraeli? No, he merely footed the bill for the ridiculous extravagances of the younger son of a Scotch marquess, who repaid him by getting him sentenced to two years penal servitude. In allowing this to happen Wilde not only ruined himself and his family, but completely betrayed the "Art" he had so often and so ostentatiously proclaimed to be the dearest thing in the world to him. He gave the British Philistine his most resounding triumph and at a stroke undid the patient work of two generations. The hatred of art, which is one of the few genuine emotions of the English-speaking peoples, was immensely fortified. It may be said of him that he contributed to prolong the barbarity of nations.

But I cannot leave Wilde on this note of condemnation, just though I believe it to be. The savagery of his sentence and punishment (scientifically worked out to break body and spirit of a ruthless and physically tough criminal) and the horrible public persecution to which he was subjected, are really topics for the psychologist of sadism, lynching, and mob terrorism. For the victim one can only feel indignation and pity. Nobody was made a whit the happier or more "moral" by this brutality; there was simply a great increase in hypocrisy and cant, and posterity was deprived of the mature work of a very distinguished writer. It is not correct to put Wilde among the great writers. Compare him with his masters in poetry, Keats, Arnold, and Gautier; with his masters in prose, Ruskin, Pater, and Flaubert—Wilde's inferiority is instantly recognizable. But it is impossible not to feel that so violent a reaction on the part of society and its legal representatives showed that there was something as wrong with that society as with its prisoner.

6

Walter Pater

Use of the word "Victorian" to describe the period 1837–1900 is convenient but misleading—an emotional label is attached to what should be only a date. Everyone has a general if inaccurate idea of what he means by "Victorian," above all whether he uses the word disparagingly or otherwise. When Lytton Strachey called his book *Eminent Victorians* he did not mean to imply admiration; but today, after a second and most disastrous war, most of us are likely to look back upon the "Victorian" age nostalgically, as a golden epoch of wealth, power, and tranquillity. In any event it is misleading to apply the adjective to men who expended their energy in criticizing their age or who, as is the case with Pater, turned their backs on it and tried to create a more sympathetic environment in the imagination. The whole of Pater's life was passed in the Queen's reign, yet he was never once summoned to Court, as the most fastidious aesthete of the time, to give his opinion on any matter connected with art or literature. Indeed it is a question, worthy the attention of some future Sir Thomas Browne: whether Queen Victoria had ever heard of Walter Pater?

Yet in appearance at least Pater was a product of his age. Over the signature of an Oxford undergraduate there exists a caricature which in its undistinguished way tells the more depressing truths about Pater's physical appearance. Here is *Marius the Epicurean* (the drawing's caption) in top hat, high stiff collar, starched cuffs, patent leather boots, morning coat, and striped trousers. This, you would instantly say, must be Podsnap junior on his way to the City, or, at best, some debilitated cavalry officer in mufti. But no! this heavily

Introduction to *Walter Pater, Selected Works* (London: William Heinemann, 1948; Duell, Sloan & Pearce, 1948).

moustached figure, the embodiment apparently of bourgeois philistinism, was that mysterious Brasenose don who dwelt in aesthetic surroundings, the Epicurean whose mental life was seemingly a series of delightful "escapes" from drab reality among sensations and ideas the least amenable to "Victorian" morals and manners.

On the face of it this looks a promising topic for a biographer—the ugly duckling of King's School, Canterbury, who turned out to be Brasenose's swan though not Leda's; or, better still, the Trojan cart-horse who smuggled Franco-German aestheticism into High Church Oxford. But, as a matter of fact, the hope is delusive, for Pater was never in any danger of connecting himself with a life drama. He was far too fastidious and timid ever to enter on a course of action which would involve the risk of a melodramatic crash, such as befell his most notorious disciple, Oscar Wilde. In accordance with the precept of his master, Epicurus, Pater "hid his life," but on the whole he is a mystery man without a mystery. If, as Wright claims, Pater went about "in a kind of disguise" there was nothing dangerous hidden behind it. The rulers of Oxford seem to have decided that he was undesirable but comparatively harmless, and the most he had to endure was the negative persecution of frustration and such nagging caricature as is likely to befall anyone who specializes in a subject so unpopular as aesthetics.

In the absence of any collection of Pater's letters or of any reminiscences of his early life which seem accurate and trustworthy, writers have naturally been tempted to look for biographical hints in his own works. Thus *The Child in the House, Emerald Uthwart, Marius the Epicurean,* and *Gaston de Latour* are all thought to contain Pater's recollections of his childhood and youth. Taken literally, the impression derived from these scattered hints would imply an imposing background of impoverished aristocrats living in old manse houses. Unfortunately for the illusion, there have been published photographs of the houses in which Pater's early life was spent, and they all turn out to be small drab suburban villas.

But for the fact that his grandfather re-emigrated to England in indignation over the war of 1812, Pater would have been born an American; and as a matter of plain fact at the time of Walter's birth (August 4th, 1839) his father was one of two brothers practicing as surgeons in the Commercial Road, Stepney. The child was only five when his father died, and the impoverished widow and children moved to a small house at Enfield, where the boy was brought up by women, among whom his grandmother is thought to have come first in his affection, on the strength of this remark in *Gaston*:

the old grandmother died, to the undissembled sorrow of Gaston, bereft unexpectedly it seemed of the gentle creature, to whom he had always turned for an affection that had been as no other, in its absolute incapacity of offence.

What a curious person Pater was! Did he suppose that a child's grief could be either pretended or dissembled, and that the chief charm of a grandmother lies in the fact that she is not offensive?

February by a coincidence was often the month which produced such events as there are in Pater's life. It was in February 1853 that he entered King's School, Canterbury, and appears to have suffered from the rough and tumble of Public School life in those days. Two reminiscing school-fellows report that Pater always evaded snow fights, and hid miserably shivering on a stone stairway. Apparently this did not preserve him from violence resulting in serious injury, if we may believe a story told by Wright with circumstantial accuracy.

In the autumn of this year (i.e., 1856) there occurred to Pater a serious misfortune. As we have seen, he had never been popular at school, and one day, for a reason not known—perhaps for no particular reason—a number of boys set upon him near the Norman Staircase; and in the midst of the scuffle a ruffianly boy, whose name may be omitted, gave Pater a dreadful kick, with the result that he had at once to be conveyed home, where he lay ill for many weeks. Mr. Wallace (i.e., *the headmaster*) having been informed of the name of the offender, not only took the matter up, but expressed his determination to expel him (i.e., *the ruffianly boy*) from the school. From Pater, however, on his sick bed came an earnest request that the boy might be forgiven, and the affair passed over. This magnanimity affected Mr. Wallace even to tears, and as late as two years after, when bidding Pater farewell, he told him that he had not forgotten "that beautiful act of Christian Charity"; while Pater's magnanimity became one of the prized traditions of the school. From the results of this lamentable occurrence, however, he never, it has been assumed, really recovered, and the peculiarity of his gait which marked him all the rest of his life is attributable to it.

If this story is true (and though it comes from Wright it sounds authentic) then it explains a good deal about Pater which seems odd and even a little repulsive. At the time of this misfortune he was an abnormally sensitive boy of sixteen, with that feeling of insecurity so often found in orphans. He was moreover in a vulnerable phase of his life, for he had recently discovered that he could write, and in the first fine careless rapture was pouring out poems, essays, and stories almost daily. (That he was incautiously showing and reading these things to other boys would explain the attack, nothing being so infuriating to the young barbarian as artistic talent.) Wright evidently thought that permanent physical injury of a particularly unfortunate kind resulted. But the psychological damage must have been even worse. Doubtless it did not cause but it must have fortified his unhappy and even furtive timidity (so excessive that Pater could never look another man in the eye), his aloofness, his inability to give himself unreservedly, and even that nostalgic longing to escape into an ideal world.

If Canterbury accidentally did Pater this injury, Canterbury provided him with an opportunity to live the only kind of life in which serenity was possible for him. In 1858 he won a scholarship of sixty pounds a year tenable for three years at Queen's College, Oxford; to which his school added a gift of thirty pounds to buy books. The suggestion has been made that the influence of Oxford on Pater was unfavorable, and that he would have been better served by "going through the mill of Fleet Street." Now, it is true that at Oxford Pater met with a good deal of opposition and even unfriendliness, as the expression of his genius developed and showed its fundamental hostility to the conventional Church life of the place, but Fleet Street would have been far worse; it would have done to his mind what Canterbury brutality did to his body and psyche. Undoubtedly Fleet Street would have cured him of his preciosity, his dilatory and over-scrupulous method of writing, his pleasure in scholarship, his dilettantism; but in curing him it would have destroyed him. You could not make that silk purse into a sow's ear, Walter Pater into George Augustus Sala. Oxford was the only possible haven.

Pater still had before him six or seven years of poverty and uncertainty about a career when he went up to Oxford as a freshman in October, 1858. He was also struggling with a crisis in religious faith, which was a common enough experience in those days and left its mark on many who broke away from orthodoxy. Many English writers of the time were essentially lay preachers, *curés manqués*, bishops who missed the ecclesiastical bus. Carlyle, Ruskin, Arnold, Huxley, Tyndall—they all preached. And if Pater wrote with such extreme care, such attention to maintaining the tone of a decent urbanity, it was largely because he was determined not to preach, not to exhort, not to condemn, not to proselytize, not to force unasked advice on the nation. While Pater was at Canterbury he had been noted (we are informed) for religious fervor, but may not his masters and pastors have been mistaken in the quality of this devotion? Doubtless this piety existed, but it was aesthetic rather than spiritual, appreciative certainly, but fundamentally lacking in conviction. Whatever his subsequent hesitations and compunctions and turnings back, Pater could never have been a Christian such as, in their various ways, were Newman and Stanley, Arnold and Jowett.

In connection with Pater's religious views while at Canterbury, it is tempting to quote the passage from *Gaston de Latour* about Gaston and his friends as they "served" the bishop at mass, where Pater describes them as "zealous, ubiquitous, more prominent than ever, though for the most part profoundly irreverent" and notes their "disdain of the untonsured laity." Whether intended or not the whole passage (in Chapter 2 of *Gaston*) could pass as a description of the Canterbury King's Scholars during service, even down to the touch of snobbery at the end. And the phrase "profoundly irreverent" may remind us that at this very period of supposed religious fervor the youthful Pater was delighting in the works of Voltaire. Then, turning over the pages of *Marius the Epicurean* we light upon the passage where Marius reads the works of "that Voltaire of antiquity," Lucian of Samosata,

writings seeming to overflow with that intellectual light turned upon dim places, which, at least in seasons of fair mental weather, can make people laugh where they have been wont, perhaps, to pray.

It must be remembered that Oxford was, among other things, a seminary for the higher clergy, and even such unlikely persons as Morris and Burne-Jones originally went up with the intention of taking holy orders. Pater's two school friends, who matriculated about the same time, both became clergymen, and it seemed the obvious career for a poor clever youth who had won a scholarship. But these very school friends, who must have been most nearly acquainted with Pater's real views, were scandalized when he said he intended to take holy orders. Both declared that they would protest to the bishop, and one instantly cut Pater.

Pater did not suffer without regret this separation from an ancient creed which had lost its meaning, and a close friend who turned out to be a bigot. His mood was one of wistful uncertainty, of the mind at unwilling war with cherished feelings. Yet with Voltaire to banter him out of the old ways and Goethe to console him with love of art, serenity, curiosity, Pater had not much to regret. He always sympathized instinctively with men who had lived at epochs of great mental change—the age of the Antonines, the Renaissance. Remembering these early troubles and self-questionings we can see how easily he could in their case follow his favorite practice of identifying himself with the mind about which he was writing.

On the material side, this repudiation by his friends brought complications and anxieties, for if he did not take holy orders, how was Pater to live? Outwardly, he lived calmly, forming new friendships and travelling on the Continent, particularly in Germany, then the country of his admiration. He was also lucky enough to attract the attention of Jowett who, as Professor of Greek, offered to give extra lectures in Greek free of charge to any of the men sufficiently interested to attend. No fewer than three attended, and Pater was one of them.

Now, whatever success Jowett achieved as an unorthodox churchman, a teacher of Greek and trainer of future pro-consuls, and a sort of concealed dictator of the University, he was not inspired as a guide of perplexed and sensitive intellectuals. He greatly disliked the aesthetic movement, and did all he could to discourage young men from it. Thus, for a whole year, he tormented young Addington Symonds by forcing him to give up the work he really liked in order to translate a heavy German metaphysician. And it was probably Jowett's influence which directed young Pater's reading away from pure literature to metaphysics, with the result that he took only second-class honors.

This comparative failure naturally brought up in a very acute form the question what the new graduate was to do for a living? In view of the evidence as to Pater's real views, it is certainly a little startling to find that with a Renaissance light-heartedness he applied for ordination to the Bishop of London. Apparently the application would have succeeded, and Pater would have spent his life as a country parson, a kind of aesthetic Naaman in the house of a philistine Rimmon, but for the two school friends already mentioned. At the first hint of the news they instantly began a feverish correspondence of protest with the Bishop, and induced others to do likewise. The application was refused, and Pater's "friend" McQueen, a wealthy young man, who led this opposition, virtuously retired and bought himself an estate, leaving Pater to face the awkward problem of earning bread and butter and a roof.

At this crisis, another misfortune occurred. The aunt who

had looked after the Pater children since the death of their parents and grandmother, herself died suddenly in Dresden; and thus at twenty-two Pater found himself alone and poor, without a profession, and with two dependent sisters. Unfortunately, we have practically no information covering the important period, December 1862 to February 1864. Had Pater been left any private means? What provision had been made for his sisters? How did he dispose of the girls during that time? What plans, if any, did he make for his own career? All we are told is that "for a couple of years he lived in lodgings in High Street, and took pupils." Cramming the stupid and lazy must have been a come-down for one trying to live up to Goethe's lofty standards of self-culture. But in the end all was well—on the 5th February, 1864, Pater was elected a probationary Fellow of Brasenose, an appointment made permanent a year later. Perhaps Jowett's secret influence was behind this, but all we are told is that Pater owed this essential step in his fortunes to "his knowledge of Hegel."

Once inside this snug haven Pater was extremely careful to take every precaution against being intrigued out of it, as he had been intrigued out of taking holy orders. Apparently there were no love affairs in Pater's life; or, if there were, they were conducted with such supernatural discretion (whether male or female) that they never got into print or even into traditional gossip. The only real danger of deprivation he ever ran was when he published one of the most civilized books which appeared in England in his lifetime. At all events, by 1869 Pater felt sufficiently secure to bring his sisters to a house in Bradmore Road, Oxford. Even before that his life had settled into a routine which lasted with little change until 1880. Until 1880 he was Tutor of his College, and in any case was always in Oxford during term. During vacations he travelled on the Continent with his sisters or with some University friend, such as Shadwell (the future Provost of Oriel) or A. H. Sayce, the orientalist. Germany was now replaced by Italy and France. All of which gives a somewhat ironic point to Pater's famous dictum that "failure is to form habits."

In 1860 Pater destroyed his early writings, and such fragments as have survived in Wright's biography do not give us the slightest reason to regret the sacrifice. For some years afterwards Pater apparently wrote little or nothing, but began again as soon as he had achieved the security and periods of leisure given by his fellowship. "Diapheneité," his first acknowledged piece, was written in July 1864, and his first publication was the essay on Coleridge which appeared in the *Westminster Review* for January 1866. This was followed by "Winckelmann" (*Westminster Review*, January 1867); "Notes on Leonardo da Vinci" (*Fortnightly Review*, November 1869); and "Sandro Botticelli" (*Fortnightly Review*, August 1870). The study of William Morris called "Aesthetic Poetry," though written in 1868, was not published until 1889, and for some reason withdrawn from later editions of *Appreciations*. Not until February 1873 did Pater collect some of his essays into a small book, rather unwisely entitled *Studies in the History of the Renaissance*. The title given to later editions, *The Renaissance, Studies in Art and Poetry*, is much more accurate, and if used at first might have protected Pater from some of the hostile criticism he had to endure.

Carefully and slowly as Pater had proceeded, cautiously as he had phrased his views, this book was instantly assailed with that hostility which greets all who run counter to accepted prejudices, particularly those few who in an English-speaking country are bold enough to claim an importance for the arts and the intellectual life above mere pastime and idling. The book's title was particularly unfortunate, for Pater's purpose was not to relate history but to present a series of imaginative reconstructions of Renaissance personalities. The book throughout repudiated the abstract metaphysical approach to art of the Hegelians and the ethical views of Ruskin; while the "Conclusion" is an eloquent if (in view of Pater's position) indiscreet statement of the author's "Cyrenaicism." (See pp. 84–86.)

If war should be suspended long enough for the academic world to return to its habits of otiose research, it might do a service to the world of letters by collecting relevant extracts from the first reviews of famous books. Those which I have been able to collect about Pater's *Renaissance* seem to conform to the usual impertinence and folly of hasty first impressions. The anonymous critic of Blackwood's thought the interpretation of Botticelli's Madonnas "one of the most incongruous and grotesque misinterpretations ever invented by man." Mrs. Mark Pattison, perhaps assisted by her husband, the querulous not to say pedantic Rector of Lincoln College, naturally pounced on the unjustified claim of the title, and wrote:

We miss the sense of the connection between art and literature and the other forms of life of which they are the outward expression, and feel as if we were wandering in a world of unsubstantial dreams.

But the real offense of the book was not in these things, whether the critics were correct or not, but in the originality of Pater's temperament, the civilized quality of his mind and personality. Arthur Symons goes to the point when he says of this book:

Here was criticism as a fine art, written in prose which the reader lingered over as over poetry, modulated prose which made the splendour of Ruskin seem gaudy, the neatness of Matthew Arnold a mincing neatness, and the brass sound strident in the orchestra of Carlyle.

And the really dangerous enemy made by *The Renaissance* was the once friendly Jowett. This cherubic Cato could not have viewed Pater's "Cyrenaicism," his Goethe-and-Gautier aestheticism, with anything but abhorrence. Contrast their opinions on the aim and conduct of life. Says Pater:

Well, we are all *condamnés*, as Victor Hugo says . . . we have an interval, and then our place knows us no more. Some spend this interval in listlessness, some in high passions, the wisest in art and song. . . . Of this wisdom, the poetic passion, the desire of beauty, the love of art for art's sake has most; for art comes to you professing frankly to give nothing but the highest quality to your moments as they pass, and simply for those moments' sake.

On the other hand, Jowett had stated the whole duty of man more concisely but from a very different point of view: "Can any summary rule be given more than this, every day and every hour to frame yourself with a view to getting over a weakness?"

Or as Matthew Arnold rather acidly described it, "bracing the moral fibre."

Pater's courteous but unmistakable dissent from this very muscular Christianity was all the more annoying and distasteful, since in an unguarded moment the Master of Balliol had dropped one of his carefully premeditated and lapidary oracles on the topic of Pater. "I think you have a mind which will come to great eminence," he had said. And now this promising recruit had gone over to the enemy, to "art and self-indulgence." After reading Pater's *Renaissance*, the Master is said to have uttered a "stinging epigram" which unluckily has not been preserved. However deeply offended as a gentleman and a Christian, Jowett could do nothing about it at the moment; but a year later he saw his chance and took it. In 1874 came the turn of Brasenose to appoint the Junior Proctor, and Pater coveted the office (though strangely unfitted for it, one would suppose) for its prestige and extra salary. Then Jowett moved in a mysterious way, and someone else got the Proctorship. "Jowett," says A. C. Benson, "took up a line of definite opposition to Pater and used his influence to prevent his obtaining University work and appointments," adding naïvely a page or two later, "Jowett was indifferent to art, except in so far as it ministered to agreeable social intercourse."

Following this distinguished leadership, others began to view with alarm the quiet but subtle aesthete of Brasenose. Journalists now labelled him "leader of the aesthetic movement" and "hedonist," which latter word (as Pater discovered with horror) they thought meant "an immoral Greek." And in 1877 dislike and suspicion of Pater culminated in the publication of W. H. Mallock's *New Republic*.

Pater is not the sole or even chief contemporary satirized in this work, but he is attacked more vindictively and certainly with more smug contempt than any of his fellow victims. *The New Republic* is a satirical novel of talk in the manner of T. L. Peacock. Among its characters Dr. Jenkinson is meant for Jowett, Mr. Storks for T. H. Huxley, Mr. Stockton for Tyndall, Mr. Luke for Matthew Arnold, Mr. Herbert for Ruskin. Pater is "Mr. Rose the Pre-Raphaelite" (then as now a term of abuse among artists' models), "a pale creature with large moustaches" who "always speaks in an undertone, and his two topics are self-indulgence and art."

Mallock had been at Balliol and was a friend of Addington Symonds, who revised the proofs of *The New Republic*. The fact that he satirizes Jowett as well as Pater, Ruskin as well as Huxley, certainly shows impartiality. The confidence of a satirist is based on the belief that the world will agree with his scorn, and it is therefore interesting to see what an educated clever man thought the world would accept as a portrait of Pater between the *Renaissance* and *Marius*.

Mallock makes Mr. Rose-Pater scandalize his prim mixed audience by referring airily to "the shining of a woman's limbs in clear water," to the Italian Renaissance as "that strange child of Aphrodite and Tannhäuser" and "the exquisite groups and figures it reveals to us, of nobler mould than ours—Harmodius and Aristogeiton, Achilles and Patroclus, David and Jonathan, our English Edward and the fair Piers Gaveston." All this is not bad; but there is more to come.

"I look upon social dissolution" (says Mr. Rose) "as the true condition of the most perfect life. For the centre of life is the individual, and it is only through dissolution that the individual can re-emerge."

The caricature develops:

"I was merely thinking," said Mr. Rose . . . "of a delicious walk I took last week, by the river side, between Charing Cross and Westminster. The great clock struck the chimes of midnight; a cool wind blew; and there went streaming on the wild wide waters with long vistas of reflected lights wavering and quivering in them; and I roamed about for hours, hoping I might see some unfortunate cast herself from the Bridge of Sighs. It was a night I thought well in harmony with despair. Fancy," exclaimed Mr. Rose, "the infinity of emotions which the sad sudden splash in the dark river would awaken in one's mind—and all due to that one poem of Hood's!"

Later on Mr. Rose speaks in terms of horror of the ugliness of London:

Think of the shapeless houses, the forest of ghastly chimney-pots, of the hell of distracting noises made by the carts, the cabs, the carriages—think of the bustling, commonplace, careworn crowds that jostle you—think of an omnibus—think of a four-wheeler.

When I go to ugly houses, I often take a scrap of artistic crétonne with me in my pocket as a kind of aesthetic smelling-salts.

But for the fact that it is too intellectual and well-written, *The New Republic* from its point of view might have run as a serial in *Punch* with illustrations by George du Maurier. It sums up extremely well the attitude of contemporary society toward Pater, aestheticism, and indeed any art and literature not subservient to religious, commercial, and class interests. The other guests at the country house party treat each other with the respect merit always feels for money, but Mr. Rose is invariably met with the utmost rudeness, whatever he says is interrupted or brushed aside or contradicted without apology. He is accused of addressing himself to "the half-educated," with strong insinuations that he is a homosexual, while the only thing he is represented as doing with any animation is bargaining to buy a pornographic book.

How far Pater was harmed by the various types of opposition and dislike usefully symbolized by Mallock's book it is hard to say. The new edition of *The Renaissance* published in the same year certainly dropped the "Conclusion" which contained the essence of Pater's "Cyrenaicism." Pater also dropped the Italian Renaissance as a theme, except for a lecture on Raphael in 1892, and some notes on Giordano Bruno in 1889. He could never have been a popular author, for he makes considerable demands of his readers, but he was prevented by the opposition from reaching the limited audience possible for him and from enjoying the reputation to which he was entitled. He never earned more than a hundred pounds a year by his writings, and in 1893 he was the only literary celebrity not invited by Oxford University to the Shelley Memorial ceremonies. "I was not asked," he replied gently to the queries of an amazed Edmund Gosse.

Among the other misdemeanors which made Pater so much disliked by the right-thinking persons of his time was the grave offense of furnishing his college rooms "in the aesthetic style." I must confess I had imagined these as a bit florid until I happened on the memorial notes of Edward Manson (*Oxford Magazine*, 1906), who had Pater for his tutor in 1869. He thus describes the rooms:

They were panelled in a pale green tint, the floor was matted, the furniture was oak and severe in style, there were a few choice prints on the walls, choice books on the shelves, and a dwarf orange-tree with real oranges on it, adorned the table.

The people who jeered at this as decadent aestheticism, themselves inhabited drawing-rooms encumbered with ornate mahogany, flowered wall-paper, numberless gilt-framed pictures, stands and what-nots covered with an enormous clutter of objects ranging from Babylonian bricks to presents from Brighton. They really ought to have been grateful to Pater for applying in Oxford what Whistler had learned from Paris about the Japanese.

In 1880 Pater took steps to break the monotony of his life and perhaps to make a bid for respectability by resigning his tutorship to write *Marius the Epicurean*, a task which occupied him for several years, including a winter spent in Rome. Unfortunately, Pater's "hide-thy-life" principles have deprived us of any records of this Roman episode, except what may be doubtfully inferred from the pages of *Marius*. No other place in the world could have satisfied him—not even Athens—as Rome could, for in itself, its age-old traditions and history, it so strikingly embodies that complex, contradictory attitude which is the essence of both Pater's temperament and philosophy of life—a loyalty hesitating between Antiquity and Christianity, a reluctance to give up either, and a hopeless attempt, often abandoned always reviving, to find a satisfying formula in which both were harmonized.

Among the visible examples of this in Rome, Pater would notice and appreciate the fact that the Vatican contains the world's largest collection of pagan statues—"idols of the heathen" as they were bluntly but not untruly called by the "barbarian" Flemish Pope, Adrian VI. The Church, Pater saw, having overthrown and done its best to liquidate the older rival religions, had turned round and piously collected their relics. Over such amiable paradoxes he could muse for many delightful hours, unmolested by the "very objectionable people in Oxford."

Naturally, also, Pater sympathized with the point of view of the Renaissance prelates. He saw that it was not their intention to abolish the Faith which they inherited from centuries of predecessors, but somehow to incorporate with it the "culture" of earlier ages, in part the creation of their remote forefathers. Among laymen who made the attempt to reconcile these incompatibles was that Pico della Mirandola on whom Pater wrote an essay. A document in the same spirit, which Pater most certainly could have picked up in the Roman book-shops, is the *De Partu Virginis* of Sannazzaro, a most curious retelling of the Nativity story in Virgilian style and in terms of the older religions of Nature. To a man like Pater, prepared as he was to receive with docility the complex impressions of Rome, Sannazzaro's God who is also Jupiter Optimus Maximus would come to seem no stranger than the title "Pontifex Maximus" assumed by Renaissance Popes. Again, as Pater turned from the relics of the great pagan civilizations to the catacombs or the Christian Museum at the Lateran, he must have been struck by the sweetness of feeling, the ardent humanity of the early Christian inscriptions. He had only to pass from the lofty splendor of antique marbles and of sonorous classical Latin to the epitaphs with their naïve unforced expressions of tender regret and affection to recognize that something new and precious had entered human experience. Pater's own feelings were in closest harmony with the spirit of the place, and this complex of changing moods is the essence of *Marius the Epicurean* and one of the chief reasons for its perpetual charm.

Marius the Epicurean was published in two volumes in 1885. Although, like other permanent books, Marius had to wait more than a decade before the reading public discovered it, the critical reception of the book was far less hostile than that which met *The Renaissance*. There was now little or no question of burning with a clear gem-like flame and of making the aesthetic uttermost of every counted moment in a brief life without hope of resurrection. Early in the book the hedonist, Flavian (who partly represents the early Pater), is dispatched to the funeral pyre; there is a Christian knight in shining armor who from time to time rides through the pages singing an unspecified hymn; while Marius himself, abandoning at least temporarily the wicked Cyrenaics for the Stoics, dies with the last rites of the Church, owing to his last moments being spent by accident as one of a band of arrested Christians on their way to martyrdom. Prejudices of readers and critics being thus soothed, there was less acerbity, less of that grudging note which met *The Renaissance*.

Evidently Pater considered the publication of *Marius* an event of importance. To the surprise of his acquaintances, he gave up the house he had rented in Oxford since 1869, and took a house at 12 Earl's Terrace, Kensington. People who knew Pater asked themselves and each other what was the motive for this abrupt move? Was it a desire to break away from the routine of habit, which is failure in life? Or was it, as he told Richard Jackson, because "there are in Oxford some very objectionable persons from whom I would gladly separate myself"?

There is no need to doubt the sincerity of Pater's explanation, but there was doubtless another and more ambitious motive he did not care to reveal. He was now forty-five and about to publish the *magnum opus* of his life, and now or never was the time to step beyond the jealous professionalism of Oxford to a wider and worldlier audience. Now was the time for Walter Pater to emerge from his tasteful little hermitage and make advances to Society. Hence this move, hence new sartorial adventures, hence Pater's presence at what George Moore unkindly calls "the dullest houses in London." Alas, if Pater dreamed of playing the part of a respected Mr. Rose in real life, of being taken up by pluto-

cratic Society, of competing successfully with his witty fol-
lower, Wilde, he was indeed mistaken. Though he spent his
vacations in London during the years 1885 to 1893, and
"went out" with exemplary persistence, he never became a
Society celebrity. Indeed, as Wilde said on another occasion,
the very idea was "grotesque and irreligious."

In other respects the move was not without benefits, of a
more or less doubtful sort. Pater was able to see something of
his non-academic colleagues, from Moore to Wilde, from
Lionel Johnson to Arthur Symons. He wrote some signed
reviews—always a dangerous indulgence for a writer of positive gifts. He published *Imaginary Portraits*, erroneously supposed by many to be his best book; re-issued *The Renaissance* with a very slightly altered "Conclusion" restored
(perhaps as a mild defiance to the "very objectionable people" at Oxford) and recklessly began publishing *Gaston*
before he had finished it, with the result that he never did
finish it. And in 1893 he abandoned his London house and
silently returned to Oxford, defeated perhaps but not de-
pressed, to a house at 64 St. Giles'.

Since Pater appears to have kept up his customs of Continental travel, it is difficult to reconcile this increased occupation with the picture often given of him in that part of his
life as a debilitated invalid of extreme preciosity. It was said
that he breakfasted in bed and then lay in a fragile manner
propped on cushions and pillows, reading the dictionary.
Occasionally he made a convulsive effort, rose at eleven, and
delivered a lecture—to an audience of eight or ten.

It is a seductive picture, but really more worthy of the
satirical Mr. Mallock than of an official or semi-official biographer. Nevertheless it is true that at the age of fifty Pater
was already an old man whose charm had distinctly waned
and given place to a weary courtesy. Some have thought that
this weariness had grown so great that Pater had entirely
abandoned the hedonism of manhood and returned to his
boyish notion of taking holy orders. There is a story about
this which is worthy of Talleyrand:

Having heard from a common friend that Pater had "become
almost a Christian," Mr. Moorhouse ventured to enquire before

leaving (little thinking that he would never see Pater again)
whether it was true that he had seen cause to change his opinions
on religion. But Pater put by the question with a smile. "Ah,"
said he, "what discussions we used to have in those old days!"
He then spoke of Mr. Moorhouse's poems, and begged him to
continue to write hymns. "We do so much need good hymns,"
he said, "and you are just the person to write them."—(Wright's
Life of Walter Pater)

In spite of his alleged valetudinarianism, Pater was killed
only by an unexpected combination of dangerous illnesses.
In June 1894 he had rheumatic fever, and was nursed by his
sisters and the indefatigable Mrs. J. R. Green (J. A. Symonds's sister Charlotte), who seems to have made a habit
of watching over the sick-beds of Oxford heroes. Apparently
his nurses put Pater to sit by an open window before he had
recovered, with the result that he was stricken with pleurisy.
A second serious illness coming so quickly might easily have
been instantly fatal, but Pater still had the strength to rally
from the pluerisy. Unfortunately he seems not to have been
sufficiently warned about the weakness of the heart which
follows rheumatic fever. He was allowed to leave his bed-
room, for the first time after this second illness, on the 29th
July (1894), and died the next morning of heart failure. He
was buried in Holywell Cemetery, Oxford, with the inscription: *In te Domine speravi.*

Material for Pater's life is scanty and on the whole color-
less, while the suppression of his letters makes it impossible
to get very close to the man as he really was. On the other
hand, we have all the writings published during his life and
some posthumously issued work; and, after all, these writings
he has bequeathed us are all that really remain of him and
what is important to us. But, for a war-weary generation,
scrambling on somehow from day to day, Pater's work may
seem as remote as Pater's epoch. This easy cosmopolitan
travelling in time and space, this leisurely visiting of old
books, old pictures, old statues, old towns, may only raise
envy of those fabulous times when a man could take a ticket
for anywhere in Europe at a moment's notice, legally own his
old gold, and legally change it anywhere. How (I cannot

help wondering) will a generation so sorely harassed look upon the writings of one whose chief problem was how to enjoy life with intelligence and sensibility and knowledge? To apply the principle which Pater took without acknowledgment from Goethe—what do these books mean to *us*? I shall not pretend to answer that question in a sentence.

Fundamentally Pater was neither prose-poet nor critic, but something in between the two, with the critic or at any rate the man of letters predominating. The fact that good literary critics are rarer than good poets need not cause either elation or depression, and rather too much has been made of it. After all, Galapagos tortoises which are ugly are much rarer than antelopes which are very attractive. On the other hand the multitude of literary critics who are not good is enormous and oppressive, especially since they naturally rate their own ungraceful carpings above the work of people who can produce other types of writing; which results in a sort of intellectualist Gresham's Law—i.e., bad writing drives out good. Probably the happy and healthy state for arts of all kinds is neither in the monastery nor the lecture-room, but in the workshop where criticism is chiefly by emulation, and successful criticism consists in doing a good thing better.

In spite of wars and revolutions and the exigencies of the common man we still have (by what miracle?) an immense amount of art and literature inherited from the past. As long as there is any esteem for this heritage, it will need curators and critics, above all critics with the rare gifts of appreciation and interpretation. Among the defects of criticism we must deplore the acrimonious tone and the dogmatic precept—as if a critic were an eighteenth-century schoolmaster with a disordered liver and a too active cane. There have been too many fusty or frivolous pedants giving forth dogmatic rules of literary and artistic procedure in matters where they were ludicrously incompetent. To this, many gifted men in the nineteenth century added an intolerable love of preaching. Out-bidding the melancholy Jacques they saw sermons in everything, and pitilessly delivered them. Of such was the kingdom of Coleridge, Carlyle, Ruskin, and a multitude who did not possess their remarkable gifts.

Acrimonious criticism is a kind of literary cock-fighting, and one can only deplore the fact that a luminous poet like Pope should have wasted so much time, ability, and nervous energy on a purely negative work, *The Dunciad*. The retaliation no doubt was richly deserved, but it only immortalized the people it was supposed to destroy.

The criticism of precept may be traced far back through European writing to the *Poetics* of Aristotle, a work in some respects of extraordinary merit, though it contains statements of very doubtful validity, and abounds in *vérités à la Palisse*, including two whole sections on the most elementary facts of speech and grammar. With Aristotle analytic generalization tends to become precept, and instead of saying "this is what the poets do," he says or implies "this is what poets ought to do." From this arose the belief in rules and the "critic" in the rôle of a birch-bearing dominie whose duty it was to flog erring creative writers. Hence the brutalities of the old *Quarterly*, Edinburgh and Blackwood's, of Jeffrey and Gifford, Croker and Lockhart, "this-will-never-do," "back-to-your-gallipots."

A quite different tendency may be traced to "Longinus," who showed clearly that the aim of literature (and of the other arts) is to give intellectual pleasure, and hence that no art needs to be justified by supposed secondary utilities. Quality is determined, not by rules and experts, but by the response of the audiences for whom the specific work is intended, and this is not the result of following formulas but of gifted and powerful personalities. Thus "Longinus" (whoever he was) started the opposite kind of criticism—the criticism of enthusiasm, appreciation, interpretation, showing what is admirable rather than what is supposed to need reprehension. The object of "Longinus" is not critical legislation but the attainment and sharing of the highest forms of intellectual enjoyment. Above all, he avoids wasting time on such flimsy paradoxes as Aristotle's arguments to prove that poetry is "more serious and scientific" than history.

Though Pater was obviously of the party of "Longinus," he never quotes him as far as I recollect, while he often quotes Aristotle and was much influenced by Platonic ideas.

The chief influence on Pater was not any writer of antiquity, but Goethe. Though hardly a professional critic, Goethe could not speak or write on any topic of art and literature without hitting off some vivid suggestion, some highly important and profound remark. His criticism is all the better for being mostly free from the apparatus and pretense of formal criticism, especially as he tends always to raise the subject from specialist and pedantic interests to a wide, serene world of universal culture. Informal criticism has produced some of the critical masterpieces of our own literature—the "defenses" of poetry by Sidney and Shelley, the Francis Thompson essay on Shelley, Wordsworth's and Arnold's prefaces, and, more recently, the slangy, erratic, but highly original remarks on American Literature by D. H. Lawrence.

Pater had a great, perhaps exaggerated admiration for Charles Lamb, and some have been tempted to write of them as kindred spirits. There is something in this, but in so many ways Pater was more akin to the solitary genius of Thomas Gray who might have stood among the highest of our critics (in the widest and best sense), for it is clear from his Letters and fragmentary notes that he anticipated Rousseau and even Goethe. We may lament Gray's indolence and streak of foppishness, but the fact is he suffered all the loneliness of a man too far ahead of his time. After the death of West and the never really healed breach with Walpole, he had no one to write for until he met Bonstetten, and then it was too late. If Pater was forced to "hide his life," what compulsion to do so must there have been on Gray in that chauvinist, philistine, purse-proud, pedigreed society of the eighteenth century? Gray had probably even more reasons for sheltering in Peterhouse and Pembroke than Pater for "hiding his life" behind the walls of Brasenose.

There are two important differences between Gray and Pater, which determined their lives as writers. The writing and publication of his poems satisfied the creative impulse in Gray and whatever literary ambition he may have had, but he lacked some point of concentration for all the learning and sensitive appreciation and genuine discovery which did not find expression in verse. In Pater the frustrated poet gives color and warmth to his prose, while his duties as coach and tutor supplied him with form and motive for the expression of his "sensations and ideas." It was the unsatisfied poet in Pater who gradually developed essays into "imaginary portraits," or "prose idylls" as he would have liked to call them.

Pater had laid down the principle that: "To regard all things and principles of things as inconstant modes or fashions has more and more become the tendency of modern thought."

And again: "What we have to do is to be forever curiously testing new opinions and courting new impressions, never acquiescing in a facile orthodoxy."

Now, it would seem as if the intellectuals of this century had set out to burlesque Pater's ideas by applying them too literally. This "regarding all things as fashions" and "ever courting new impressions" has turned the palace of art into a giant Aesthetic Fun Fair, where newer and wilder exhibits vie with one another, and a jaded if impecunious public calls incessantly for bigger thrills and cleverer titters. Among the exhibits and side shows have been Russian novelists and American poets, Muscovite ballets and Studio 28 films, African idols and Mexican mosaic masks, Japanese novels and Chinese poems, "Les Chants de Maldoror" and "Frankie and Johnny," Brancusi's sea-shore eggs and Henry Moore's calamitous excrescences. Painting has been a vertiginous harlequinade of Impressionists, Post-Impressionists, Fauves, Futurists, Cubists, Vorticists, Expressionists, Abstractionists, Surrealists, and music has ranged from the tortured pigs of Stravinski's "Sacre" to the jig-a-jig of Jellyroll Morton's Red Hot Peppers, while the whole Fun Fair shakes and stamps to the inescapable crescendos of Ravel's "Boléro."

Voilá où mènent les mauvais chemins. After decades of this fracas, it will do none of us any harm to turn aside and enter a quiet lecture room and listen to a gentle voice speaking of the European tradition. As long as our aircraft-carrier island remains (unfortunately) anchored off the misty north-western shores of Europe, and any breathing space is granted for the living of life and not a mere scramble to survive, the study of the influences which have built

civilization as we know it or aspire to it will lie chiefly within
the areas marked out by Pater's interests. Pater certainly did
not wish (as the quotations just made show) that these
should remain static, a body of orthodoxy to which no
additions or alterations must be made, a republic of letters
which is forbidden to annex new territory. But the prudent
use he made of his own principles of "fashions" and "courting new impressions" is a testimony to his good sense and
good taste, his "divine moderation." Without it there is
always the chance that the republic of art and letters may
collapse into totalitarian regimes labelled Journalism or Politics.

If we believe that there is a genuine difference between a
"culture-complex" (which means any group functioning as
gregarious tool-making animals) and "civilization" (which
means humanely-ordered men seeking finer ways of feeling
and living), then the world of Walter Pater has much to
offer us. The virtues and vices of "class" are a delusion. Any
mob of any class or of all classes mixed, when it is a mob,
will tend to the same collective distractions of racing, gam-
bling, alcohol, all crude sensations at their rawest. You end
up by deifying half-witted criminals and bottom dogs. And if
you join the Aesthetic Fun Fair, in the end you will find
yourself calling for the identical raw crudities—is it not the
super-highbrow who prefers the detective story to the novel,
jazz to music, and *Helzapoppin* to *Henry* V?

Pater's reasonableness in the choice of themes thus
avoided provincial nationalism on the one hand and the
dangers of too much cosmopolitan change of fashion on the
other hand. There was a danger here. If the uneducatable
live in an ever shrinking circle of what touches only themselves, and the over-educated exhaust their sensibilities by
too frantic a search for novelties, may not a mind like Pater's
end up by refusing to accept anything new, and settle into a
narrow orthodoxy of accepted masterpieces? As we already
have seen, just that accusation was made against Pater; i.e.,
that in his later years he lay in bed till noon reading only the
dictionary—*La chair est triste, hélâs, et j'ai lu tous les livres*.
How can that be reconciled with his increased production

and friendship with younger men like Moore and Wilde, Symons and Lionel Johnson?

It was of course Pater's temperament which saved him from both academic dullness and avant-garde excesses. His personality had all the obstinate strength of the timid when pressed upon too heavily. His serenity, his cheerfulness, his fastidious good taste, his eagerness to put before us the best he has discovered—these qualities may prevent him from reaching the great heights but save him also from the excesses and defects so obvious in his contemporaries, Carlyle and Arnold, Ruskin and J. A. Symonds. Certainly these writers produced passages and aspirations more thrilling than anything Pater wrote, but unlike them he never forgot that "the aim of culture is not rebellion but peace."

Certainly this temperament of Pater's was pleasure-loving, or, if you agree with the prim lady in *The New Republic*, "self-indulgent," but not in the ordinary sense. The pleasures and indulgences were intellectual and aesthetic, and the delight of the senses was to be restrained and decorous, with aestheticism by no means excluding asceticism of a comely sort. It was Pater who picked from Gautier's writings a phrase which the minor aesthetes soon wore out by their incessant application of it to themselves—"he was one for whom the visible world existed." The pleasure of the eye formed a large part of Pater's philosophy of enjoyment, but this aestheticism, this ever-renewed joy in the changing beauty of things did not close up for him the seemingly rival and hostile worlds of philosophy and religion. But to attract Pater philosophy and religion must be beautiful—he would not drink the water of wisdom or the wine of salvation from an old tin mug. Philosophy must not be presented in arid ponderous treatises, but in some golden dialogue of Plato. How characteristic of Pater and of his personal interpretations that he applied to Plato that phrase of Gautier I have just quoted, and that he contrived to find in the text of the dialogues authority for the view that Plato too believed in art for art's sake!

But religion? Here, especially in his own time, Pater's temperament left him peculiarly open to misunderstanding and censure. Now of course people will either shrug off religion contemptuously and hence be unwilling to concede its importance in Pater's life, or, if they take it seriously, will certainly be indignant at the notion that religion may be a matter of "mere" aesthetic preference. How personal Pater's views were, how much he was accustomed to read his own views and tastes into even the greatest characters, may be judged from the fact that in *Marius* he speaks gravely of "the divine moderation of Our Lord," a view which Henry James instantly noted and denounced. Yet this disposition to look on religion as an aesthetic spectacle in which one may take part without yielding the ceremony any real belief certainly dated back to Pater's days in Canterbury. While he was feeding his scepticism with Voltaire and his neo-Hellenism with Goethe, he could not help delighting in the grandeur of the cathedral, feeding upon the ritual and the music, the jewelled windows and the great memories of the past, the sculptured stones and the eloquence of Arthur Stanley.

Late in life Pater tried to renew these sensations by attending the services, of a highly ritualistic kind, performed by a company of extremely opulent curates who called themselves Augustinians and functioned in the East End. Their leader, who dubbed himself "Father" Nugée (a disquieting old bird from the look of his photograph) censured this frivolity by saying pointedly: "We don't want mere sight-seers." To which Pater instantly replied: "The Church of England is nothing to me apart from its ornate services." There you have it in a phrase.

In Pater's day—and we cannot claim that it is much better today—there were a harshness and dullness, a brutality about everyday living blandly sanctioned by business and politics, religion and law. From the cruel squalor of the slums, the banal ordinariness of comfort-worshipping suburbs, the tasteless opulence of palaces, Pater turned in despair, trying to build for himself a nook and a dream of comeliness and serenity—thereby arousing the ire of the godly and the devotion of gifted youth. That Pater was nevertheless forced to dress as a *croquemort* to avoid disturbances is one more proof of the strength of the eternal opposition—now to be found wearing utility clothing in a pre-fabricated house under a drizzle of statistics.

This shrinking from the world's ugliness and concentration on every radiant experience makes one think of the motto on Hazlitt's sundial which recorded only sunny hours —*nil nisi horas serenas numero*. The persuasive exposition of this doctrine undoubtedly was dangerous to the reckless and frivolous among Pater's disciples who took the doctrine too literally, and ignored Pater's urging of the necessity, the equal beauty, of discipline, *ascêsis*, "a girding of the loins." It was fatal to Wilde, if it really did have the effect on him he claims in *De Profundis*.

It led Pater himself into generalities of doubtful validity. He says, "the essence of humanism is . . . that belief that nothing which has ever interested living men and women can wholly lose its vitality." But the Italian humanists expressed no such view, and we may well ask to what extent facts justify this wide assumption. The quotation comes from the essay on Pico, to whom Pater could not help attributing his own views. And while Pater would no doubt have admitted, did admit regretfully, that you cannot serve Christ and Aphrodite too, or feel an equal reverence for the nymphs and the saints, still he had always a fellow feeling for those who attempted the impossible syncretism. Like the men of the Renaissance, Pater wanted to make the best of both religious worlds, to run with the pagan hare and hunt with the Christian hounds. He asserts, for instance, that the pagan poetry of Provence only yields its full flavor in a Christian setting. But the idea runs through much of Pater's work, even in Hellenism, when he balances an exposition of the Bacchanals by a eulogy of hard Lacedaemon.

The situation occurs so often in Pater's work because it was an essential part of his temperament, exasperating to his enemies and baffling to his friends, whom it sharply divided. Frank Harris and George Moore see only the pagan side of Pater, because that is all they want to see. For the same reason, more or less pious Oxford friends were ready to believe that eventually Pater was converted and ripe for holy orders and a canonry. No doubt he would have accepted them, if offered, but in the spirit of that Renaissance prelate who is alleged to have inserted in his crucifix an antique cameo of the Foamborn.

Hence it is that Pater came to dwell so affectionately upon epochs of sudden and perplexing change in intellectual and religious things—the Renaissance and the age of the Antonines. Hence, too, his pre-occupation with fancies about the gods in exile. The idea came to him, of course, from Heine, but Pater was seldom more happily inspired than when he slowly distilled, in *Denys l'Auxerrois*, a legend of the return of Dionysus to the ways of men in the Middle Ages. The companion piece, *Apollo in Picardy*, is said to have been inspired by an old engraving of a picture by Domenichino, but is less happy in its result.

"Imaginary portraits," "prose idylls"—somehow they suggest a prose counterpart to Browning's *Men and Women*. But Browning hides behind a scrupulous objectivity, while so often Pater cannot refrain from projecting himself into those he was portraying. To be "neither for God nor for his enemies" is certainly a striking characteristic of Pater, but does it really apply to Botticelli and his Madonnas? Perhaps Pater had not lived long enough in Italy to know that "the Botticelli Madonna" is still a rare but persistent type of feminine beauty in Italy, with just the same delicate face, wistful refinement and melancholy grace. What the face meant to Botticelli can only be guessed, but he was certainly painting from models whose type yet remains.

Again, just ten years after Edmond de Goncourt's book had brought Watteau permanently back into fashion, Pater wrote *A Prince of Court Painters* which ends with the now famous words: "He had been a sick man all his life. He was always a seeker after something in the world that is there in no satisfying measure, or not at all."

The first sentence is true—Watteau suffered from tuberculosis. The second sentence is a perfect summing up of Walter Pater, but there is little in the records of Watteau's life or in his paintings to suggest that it has any truth at all so far as he was concerned. In the case of an imaginary character, Marius, it was legitimate to give him Pater's horror of snakes and Pater's remorse about his dead mother, but it is carrying the "prose idyll" idea too far when personal traits and whims are attributed to historical characters. When Henry James picked on that phrase in *Marius* about the "divine moderation of Our Lord" he put his finger on a weakness in Pater which must not be concealed. We must always remember that Pater's "portraits" are deliberately named "imaginary."

It is also characteristic of Pater that he builds his portraits generally round "documents," a picture or a poem or one or more translations. "Leonardo da Vinci" works up to and then gradually down from the ornate and rhetorical passage about Mona Lisa. "Joachim du Bellay" is built round the charming little lyric translated from Navagero ("A *vous, troupe légère. . . .*"), which is more characteristic of the Pléïade in general than of du Bellay in particular—a grave and sometimes satirical poet. "Pascal," even, centers round the selection of translated *Pensées* which fills two or three of its pages; and even behind Sebastian van Storck one feels Pater's paraphrasing of Spinoza.

Pater is a master of prose translation, and no one should miss the perfectly chosen passages from *Aucassin and Nicolette* and *Amis and Amile* which are the foundation stones of *Two Early French Stories*. Again, the "Demeter and Persephone" is based on a subtle counterpoint of translated passages from the Homeric Hymns, the *Thalysia* of Theocritus, Ovid's *Fasti* and Claudian's *Rape of Persephone*. And it is hardly necessary to point out how much *Marius* owes to the Cupid and Psyche episode from the *Metamorphoseon* of Apuleius, and to skilful *pastiches* of Marcus Aurelius, Fronto, and Lucian.

Marius the Epicurean affects the form of a novel, but the reader who takes it too literally as such is likely to be disappointed. It should be read as the greatest and most ambitious of Pater's prose idylls, an imaginary portrait of which we may say what was said of Flaubert's *Salammbô*, that "the pedestal is too big for the statue." In the case of *Marius* this does not matter much, for Pater was mostly concerned with his own sensations and ideas, and little enough with the actions and character of Marius, who is an abstraction only more animated than the impossible Cornelius. Take *Marius* as a story and you must be disappointed, probably bored. It should be taken as a survey of religions and philosophies from Heraclitus of Ephesus to Christian Rome, of imperial Roman society at the moment when it was at its best under the rule of the most philosophical Emperor. It is a "survey of culture" at one of those decisive changing points in Europe's life, so fascinating to one who was himself "wandering between two worlds." It was a strange way to amuse the subscribers to Mudie's Library, but unlike the usual wares peddled from that establishment it was a contribution to English literature.

The chapters of *Gaston de Latour* can be detached and read as separate essays. This is scarcely true of *Marius*, yet perhaps the book is most effective when read in brief portions of two or three chapters at a time and no more. I must dissent from the Hibernian enthusiasm of George Moore who, on reading the chapter headed "White-Nights," felt that England had at last been granted the Continental type of novelist she lacked. But it is hardly possible to read that chapter and the next one, "Change of Air," without falling under the spell of their gravely beautiful words and unworldly serenity. With exquisite skill and persuasion Pater, in his unhurried fashion, leads us to the point he wishes to make, the quotation which is the pivot of this section of the book:

If thou wouldst have all about thee like the colours of some fresh picture, in a clear light, be temperate in thy religious notions, in love, in wine, in all things, and of a peaceful heart with thy fellows.

Not to multiply instances tediously—the two chapters on Epicurean philosophy, "Animula Vagula" and (especially) "The New Cyrenaicism" can easily be detached and read apart from the rest of the book. Above all, it is essential not to rush at Pater and especially not at *Marius*—he must be read in the same detached leisurely manner he wrote.

It is probably wise to admit that Pater's work is the work of a *dilettante*—and we need not recoil from the word if we recollect that its real meaning is "one who delights in the arts and the things of the mind for their own sake." Pater wrote because writing enabled him to enjoy more fully and intelligently what he loved in the world and the creations of men's minds and hands. He was also a graceful and tactful revealer of these things to others who were willing to listen. He never scolds, never preaches, never pontificates, never sneers, never splits hairs, never patronizes, never browbeats, never wrangles. No English prose writer has better manners. He does not affect wit, and the pedantries which afflict learning and ignorance alike are alien to him. The life of the mind and of "the senses purged" was his theme, which he presents with rare gentleness and persuasion.

All Pater's books were occasionally used by him to express his own highly personal views and "philosophy," and the reader cannot help noticing that Pater is the origin (so far as England is concerned) of aesthetic views which are held to be peculiarly modern, just as in scholarship he recognized and proclaimed "the twelfth-century Renaissance" fifty years before the professional scholars. I have already spoken of his view of "all things and principles of things as inconstant modes and fashions" which has dominated aesthetic taste for so long. But it was also Pater who held the equally dangerous view that poetry is all the better for not being lucid (when did great poets write nonsense?) and that "all art tends to the condition of music," which is abstractionism. He held that:

In its primary aspect, a great picture has no more definite message for us than an accidental play of sunlight and shadow for a few moments on the wall or floor: is itself, in truth, a space of such fallen light, caught as the colours are in an Eastern carpet, but refined upon, and dealt with more subtly than by nature itself.

Dear me! How we have been crushed these thirty years and more with that "Eastern carpet" by noisy enthusiasts who certainly had no notion that they were quoting the abhorred Walter Pater. And how willing after these years of putting those ideas into practice we would treat the resulting pictures as carpets. But Pater is hardly to be blamed for this, as his shade hovers in the background murmuring in agitation, "divine moderation," "ascêsis," "burn with a clear gem-like flame."

It is natural to ask what effect Pater's work has had on other writers. His influence on the next generation—Wilde, Moore, Lionel Johnson, Yeats, Arthur Symons—is too obvious to need comment. But soon after them came the inevitable break, the reaction, and Pater went rapidly out of favor. The most successful adaptation of Pater's methods and attitude is a book which has deservedly been most widely circulated in the United States, though it seems little known in England—I mean Rachel Annand Taylor's *Leonardo the Florentine*. This poetically written book disregards the proportions and principles of an ordinary biography, to paint in brilliant hues a vast nostalgic fresco of the Italian Renaissance, a "prose Idyll" on a great scale, which should satisfy the most ardent yearning "for something in the world that is there in no satisfying measure, or not at all."

Culture—the word has become an abomination which is not made more acceptable by spelling it "kulchur" or by re-importing it in slick packages from America. We lack a word to express the idea of complete education, or civilized training of mind, muscles and senses, which was Pater's ideal. It was a rare gift which enabled him to show so vividly the charm, life, and vigor in the classics of Antiquity, when they had been made trite and worn by more than four centuries of intensive or conventional study. To take subjects which the vulgar consider "dry" and the highbrows vote "academic," and to invest them with new glamour, a wistful attractiveness, is part of Pater's achievement. When Lionel Johnson read *Plato and Platonism* and wrote: "Oh, to be reading Greats at B.N.C.," he talked like an Oxford snob, but he implied a valuable truth—that Pater was a wonderful inspirer of young men. No one who comes under his influence before the age of twenty will ever be content to remain gross and ignorant.

Every age is an age of transition, but it may be that ours is much more than this, that it is becoming one of those violent breaks with the past, with tradition, which put men into a hateful attitude of hostility and destruction to all that they have inherited—the spirit which burned the Greek lyrists at Byzantium and smashed the stained glass in Reformation England. The break of the Renaissance, though preceding and accompanying the Protestant wars of religion in the north, was intellectual and artistic, superannuating without physical violence much that had been revered and created during the millennium which went before. But if now certain world trends and pseudo-philosophies should indeed result in the ultimate violences and destructions, any surviving fragment of humanity will be too much preoccupied with the mere animal urge of survival to care or even know about "the things of the mind" which across the millennia have alike interested a Plato and a Pater. Even a less calamitous adoption of old heresy disguised as new panacea must result in a contemptuous repudiation of all that has for so many centuries formed the material of "culture," and would sweep away Pater along with many more precious things into that oblivion of destruction which befell the libraries and temples of Antiquity. Until and unless that evil time comes, Pater will hold, and under favorable circumstances greatly increase, his civilizing influence, particularly over sensitive and studious youth.

7

Jane Austen

Naturally there are differences of opinion about the merits of every author, with the usual battle between the bunkers and the debunkers; but in the case of Jane Austen, her supporters have carried it a little too far. As an example, let me cite a remark of T. B. Macaulay, of whom Lord Melbourne once remarked, "I wish to God I was half as sure about any one thing as Macaulay is about everything." Macaulay wrote:

Shakespeare has had neither equal nor second. But among the writers who, in the point which we have noticed, have approached nearest to the manner of the great master, we have no hesitation in placing Jane Austen, a woman of whom England is justly proud [essay on Madame d'Arblay].

The point which Macaulay "had noticed" is that Shakespeare "has left us a greater number of striking portraits than all other dramatists put together." From which we must infer that Jane Austen has left a greater number of striking portraits than all other novelists put together.

George Saintsbury, whose judgments are usually rather sensible and carefully graduated, went even farther in flattery. He called Miss Austen "the mother of the English novel in the nineteenth century," a remark she would have found ill-chosen; and in another book he actually says that we shall have another Homer before we see another Jane Austen. After this it seems comparatively moderate that Cardinal Newman read her novels every year "to improve his style"; that Tennyson at Lyme Regis was more interested in where Louisa Musgrove fell than in where poor Monmouth

Introduction to the Chawton Edition of Jane Austen's novels, published by Allan Wingate, Ltd., London, 1948.

landed. Arnold Bennett added a touch of the grotesque when he compared her with Zola and Thomas Hardy; while in 1902 someone published an article (I have not read it) with the modest title, *The Legend of Saint Jane*.

After gushing heroine-worship of this sort, a plain tale plainly told is likely to sound unenthusiastic. There is a legend that Queen Victoria, discussing the hereafter, observed with her usual dignity: "We shall not know Abraham." It seems more than probable that the Elliots and Bennets, Musgroves and Knightleys, even Colonel Brandon and Mr. Collins, would in real life find excuses for not "knowing" such characters as Achilles and Hamlet, Helen of Troy and Juliet. The world of Jane Austen is immeasurably distant from the robust and passionate worlds of Homer and Shakespeare, and her art is not their art. In its own way it may be perfect, but with the perfection of a Tanagra statuette compared with a temple and a cathedral.

Jane Austen's art does not aspire to splendid imaginings, high or devilish passions, great deeds and gorgeous scenes or the poetic eloquence which rises to such levels. It is an art domestic, provincial, feminine, and prosaic, placidly realist, strictly held within the author's very limited experience. Her triumph is that with all those renunciations and within those narrow limits she created novels which are enduring works of art.

The brief life of Jane Austen (16th December, 1775 to 18th July, 1817) covered a period of English history distinguished by protracted wars and by military and naval disasters transformed eventually into the triumphs of Trafalgar and Waterloo. Yet so sheltered was the privileged home population that Jane Austen's life is almost devoid of incident, while, as everybody has noticed, her novels are set in a world without war. Only after the peace do we find her pages thronged with half-pay naval officers looking for wives.

Jane Austen's mother was Cassandra Leigh, the wife of the Reverend George Austen, rector of Steventon, Hants; and Jane was their seventh child. In 1801 the family moved to Bath; in 1805 Mr. Austen died, and the survivors moved to Southampton; in 1809 they settled in the village of Chawton.

Jane never left home except on short visits, never married, was domesticated, and until 1811 wrote without encouragement, for her own amusement. The success of *Sense and Sensibility* then gave her a motive for resuming an art she had apparently ceased to practice for years. It was a life spent largely in a routine of trivial occupations among people the most ordinary and most useless. This society, which Jane Austen has anatomized with such felicitous irony, is excellently summarized by Lord David Cecil in his brilliant biography of Cowper:

"It was . . ." he says, ". . . a small world of rigid conventions and easy labours and mild amusements and regular habits, where all the men were clergymen or squires, and led much the same life whichever they were; and the women copied out extracts and played the harp; a world whose various occupations were looking after the land and sitting on the Bench and getting married, whose pleasures were sport and cards for low stakes, and small talk all the time, and now and again a ball."—[*The Stricken Deer*]

This is accurate so far as it goes, but we must remember that this society was dominated by two passions, the snobbery of rank and the snobbery of money—and since rank meant only that a family had been in possession of wealth for more than two generations, pride of purse was the dominating concern, money the criterion of excellence. Balzac is often reproached for the gusto with which he enters into the financial affairs of his characters, but he had an ardent predecessor in Jane Austen who paid particular attention to this aspect of realism. She never fails to tell us how much money her chief characters possess, and frequently in the opening sentence:

The family of Dashwood had been long settled in Sussex. Their estate was large . . . but their mother had nothing, and their father only seven thousand pounds in his own disposal.— (*Sense and Sensibility*, Chapter 1)

Mr. Darcy soon drew the attention of the room by his fine, tall person, handsome features, noble mien, and the report which was in general circulation within five minutes after his entrance, of his having ten thousand a year.—(*Pride and Prejudice*, Chapter 3)

About thirty years ago, Miss Maria Ward, of Huntingdon, with only seven thousand pounds, had the good luck to captivate Sir Thomas Bertram, of Mansfield Park, in the county of Northampton, and to be thereby raised to the rank of a baronet's lady, with all the comforts and consequences of a handsome house and large income.—(*Mansfield Park*, Chapter 1)

Emma Woodhouse, handsome, clever, and rich.—(*Emma*, Chapter 1)

Her father was a clergyman, without being neglected or poor, and a very respectable man, though his name was Richard, and he had never been handsome. He had a considerable independence, besides two good livings.—(*Northanger Abbey*, Chapter 1)

Her father was growing distressed for money. She knew, that when he now took up the *Baronetage*, it was to drive the heavy bills of his tradespeople, and the unwelcome hints of Mr. Shepherd, his agent, from his thoughts.—(*Persuasion*, Chapter 1)

Thus, at the earliest possible moment, in all Jane Austen's novels she is careful to give an exact answer to the all-important question: "How much money has he—or she—or have they?" Probably none of Jane Austen's heroines was nearer to her heart than Elinor Dashwood, none closer to her ideal of a thoroughly charming and respectable young woman. Yet Elinor is accurately acquainted with the money value of all the marriageable men, including those even whom she has no intention of considering for marriage:

"He seems a most gentlemanlike man . . ." (says John Dashwood to his sister Elinor of Colonel Brandon) ". . . and I think, Elinor, I may congratulate you on the prospect of a very respectable establishment in life."

"Me, brother—what do you mean?"

"He likes you. I observed him narrowly, and am convinced by it. What is the amount of his fortune?"

"I believe about two thousand a year. . . ."—(*Sense and Sensibility*, Chapter 33)

The position of the clergy in this cash-conscious society was not quite of such an equality as Lord David Cecil's words seem to imply. The upper ranks of the clergy, yes—but there is not a bishop, not even a canon among Jane Austen's characters. True, among the curates and vicars and rectors she knew, especially those holding the more valuable livings, were some men who were younger sons of squires with some "fortune" which they were anxious to increase by marrying young women with larger "fortunes." The Austens were hardly among these, though their "birth" was good and Mr. Austen held two livings. Socially the girls from the rectory were on an equality with the girls from the manor house, and very probably better educated, with a finer moral sense. But from the all-important aspect of "fortune" they could not compete in matrimony with young ladies whose dowries ranged from ten to fifty thousand pounds. They must therefore marry a curate or half-pay officer or some ungenteel tradesman or farmer with money or resign themselves, like Miss Austen, to a life of celibacy.

This commercial view of matrimony was accompanied, as one would expect, by extreme prudery concerning the actual relations of the sexes outside the cash nexus and social flirtation. The attitude of Jane Austen's characters toward sex is as unreal, mercenary, and gross as that of a modern Divorce Court, whose sexual ethics indeed date from that epoch. The fact that Jane Austen never married probably does not indicate a horror for the experience, but simply that she was too poor to marry the kind of man she wanted. The widow of a great painter, who incautiously married again, was heard to remark sadly: "After one has lived with an artist other men are so *boring*." Jane Austen never found her equivalent for the "artist" who would not be boring; or, if such were found, he ran away from a woman with a mind. Such has been the fate of other intellectual women.

Day dreams are forbidden to nobody, and it is interesting to note that every one of Jane Austen's novels has a Cinderella in it, a Cinderella who marries the more or less rich and handsome young man while other girls with more money and less rectory culture either have to take the wrong man or commit the enormity of elopement or (at least on one occasion) the crime of adultery. Strict attention to conventional morality, good manners, and accomplishments will (the novels imply) achieve matrimonial success, while all deviations from the code will be appropriately punished. Thus, Marianne Dashwood, though in the heroine class, rebels sufficiently against the code to be threatened by the "betrayal" of the abandoned Willoughby, and in the end must marry the "elderly" Colonel Brandon she had scorned. (This in spite of the fact that, true woman as she is, Jane Austen cannot help secretly liking such devilish rakes as Willoughby and Wickham.) On the other hand the model Elinor Dashwood is rewarded by the model Edward Ferrars, and they are happy ever after. As Jane Austen puts it, with that felicitous touch which always, or at any rate often, redeems a banal situation:

They had in fact nothing to wish for, but the marriage of Colonel Brandon and Marianne, and rather better pasturage for their cows.—(*Sense and Sensibility*, Chapter 1)

Again, Fanny Price—the heroine of *Mansfield Park*—is a penniless niece taken out of charity into the family of a baronet uncle-by-marriage. She is really a Cinderella, for after being snubbed and more or less ill-treated by her aunts for years, she wins the affections of her uncles, defeats the great heiress (Miss Crawford) and wins the Baronet's younger son, Edmund, a young man of much virtue and agreeable "fortune," though a clergyman. In *Northanger Abbey* the author set out to parody the romantic novel of Mrs. Radcliffe, and makes Catherine Morland as plain and commonplace as romantic heroines were lovely and interesting. Yet an irresistible force turns Catherine into a Cinderella, and she captures the valuable Mr. Henry Tilney. Emma Woodhouse is not a Cinderella. That part is played to perfection by the "second lead," Jane Fairfax, so poor that she was doomed to the servitude of a governess, so elegant and accomplished that even Emma felt inferior—and yet she captures young Mr. Churchill and his "fortune." Finally, in

Persuasion, the modest, younger daughter Anne unexpectedly secures the interesting Captain Wentworth.

"It was very agreeable that Captain Wentworth should be
a richer man than either Captain Benwick or Charles Hay-
ter"—who were marrying the more eligible Musgrove girls.
Anne not only receives a surprising number of proposals for
one in her position, but shows a solid heroism of constancy
in love.

"Yes. We certainly do not forget you so soon as you forget us.
It is, perhaps, our fate rather than our merit. We cannot help
ourselves. We live at home, quiet, confined, and our feelings
prey upon us. You are forced on exertion. You have always a
profession, pursuits, business of some sort or other, to take you
back into the world immediately, and continual occupation and
change soon weaken impressions."—(*Persuasion,* Chapter 23)

Strange to find Jane Austen and the Byron of *Don Juan* in
agreement.

> Man's love is of man's life a thing apart,
> 'Tis woman's whole existence; man may range
> The court, camp, church, the vessel and the mart;
> Sword, gown, gain, glory, offer in exchange
> Pride, fame, ambition, to fill up his heart,
> And few there are whom these cannot estrange;
> Men have all these resources, we but one,
> To love again, and be again undone.

So far we have been defining the conditions and limits,
some inevitable, some self-imposed, within which Jane Austen wrote. A more difficult task, perhaps never to be carried
out thoroughly, is to explain how and why it is that after a
century and a half, and the virtual extinction of the provincial society she presented and satirized, Jane Austen is still so
interesting, so readable. There are critics (probably not
themselves very successful as writers) who say that "interest"
and "readableness" are unimportant qualities, rather cheap-
jack attractions which secure frivolous readers but rather
repel the "serious." Now, if a novel is not interesting and
readable to the average non-specialist persons for whom it is
written, what on earth is the use of it? An unreadable novel,

whatever its other literary or philosophical merits, is a failure. Of course, there are changes in taste and literary fashion. Moreover, books cannot be rigidly classified into ephemeral and immortal, rubbish or works of genius. There are number-less shades of merit and limits of duration, while every decade sees very many books drop away to oblivion, a few more or less established, and perhaps one or two revived from the past. Any novelist who endures as long as Jane Austen and holds readers who are not merely academic, is entitled to respect and admiration. Her books are still alive.

Why is this? The novel of sublimated gossip is not rare, and it has been produced by generations of women more favored and sophisticated than Jane Austen, far less cramped by rigid convention and starched morality. And not one of them has really gone beyond her. Inevitably every novel carries with it the mood in which it was produced, so that a novel conceived in obedience to sterile theories and produced laboriously cannot avoid communicating the author's bore-dom. Yet gusto is not enough. A successful novelist possesses a vivid personality and the ability—innate or worked for—to express it interestingly. As well as knowing all the profes-sional business of a novelist—construction, characterization, suspense, style, and the like—he or she must be able to do more than just write cleverly about people, must indeed know how to live vicariously the lives of characters and to communicate that vitality by words. Dickens had the gift, but faults of taste; prediliction for melodrama, sentimental-ity, caricature, often caused him to betray it. In Jane Austen the gift was perhaps less vigorous, more sedate, but her taste was excellent, and she hardly ever betrayed it except under the pressure of absurd conventions.

Charlotte Brontë thought Jane Austen lacked poetry and lacked emotion, and held that her books are less true than realistic. Although the remark comes from a rival who is far less perfect as an artist, the first part of the remark at any rate is true. There is not a touch of poetry and scarcely an emotion or feeling beyond the average in all Jane Austen's work. She was a child of the sedate English eighteenth century, although she lived during that complex and exciting uprush of imaginative writing we call Romanticism. She was the contemporary of great poets and hardly knew them—what she did know of them met only cool approbation from her. She was out of sympathy with Romanticism, especially in its earlier and cruder forms. It is hard to think of Jane Austen as intellectually the contemporary of Blake, Wordsworth, Coleridge, Scott, Byron. She is nearer to Fanny Burney and Goldsmith, to Sterne even. Had she read Marivaux, one speculates? Did the knowledge of French she possessed bring her acquainted with Madame de Sévigné, with La Bruyère and La Rochefoucauld? Certainly in her novels there is an epigrammatic disillusion, bordering on worldly cynicism, which is akin to that of the caustic Duke:

Where people wish to attach, they should always be ignorant. To come with a well-informed mind, is to come with an ability of administering to the vanity of others, which a sensible person would always wish to avoid. A woman, especially, if she has the misfortune of knowing anything, should conceal it as well as she can.—(*Northanger Abbey*, Chapter 14)

Northanger Abbey was written to ridicule the excesses of Mrs. Radcliffe and other sensational romantic novelists, with their frantic appeals to sensibility and poetic emotions—the kind of novels young Shelley adored before he became a poet. In the words just quoted there is an astringent bitterness, a clear-sighted knowledge of male vanity and selfishness, almost painful in a girl of twenty-three. But La Rochefoucauld himself has not observed more keenly, generalized more truthfully and pointedly. Such remarks, often made so casually as to seem harmless, abound in Jane Austen's novels and are often pointed with satirical wit:

Mrs. Allen was one of that numerous class of females, whose society can raise no other emotion than surprise at there being any men in the world who could like them well enough to marry them.—(*Northanger Abbey*, Chapter 2)

Mr. Bennet and his sayings are too well known to bear further quotation—his "an unhappy alternative lies before you, Elizabeth," and "Let us flatter ourselves that *I* may be the survivor" must be known by hearsay to thousands who have never opened Jane Austen's novels. It is unlucky that he is a minor character and that it was never possible to repeat him.

Macaulay thinks that Jane Austen's success in presenting character is due to "touches so delicate, that they elude analysis, that they defy the powers of description, and that we know them to exist only by the general effect to which they have contributed." This is a most questionable statement, and I think every reader of Jane Austen might easily make for himself an ample collection of just those "touches" which do create character and make her writing vivid. Take, for example, this portrait of a young man:

> There were in him . . . no traits at all unusual in his sex and time of life. He was nice in his eating, uncertain in his hours; fond of his child, though affecting to slight it; and idled away the morning at billiards, which ought to have been devoted to business.—(*Sense and Sensibility*, Chapter 42)

Sometimes these "touches" are double-edged, satirizing the social snobbery of the environment as well as the victim:

> The Coles . . . very good sort of people, friendly, liberal, and unpretending; but, on the other hand, they were of low origin, in trade, and only moderately genteel.—(*Emma*, Chapter 25)

Just why an island people who owed most of their importance in the world to their success in trade should have affected to despise it is one of the laughable mysteries which make the human comedy so lamentably amusing. Jane Austen excels at double-edged satire on such anomalies, can, for instance, hit at the universal village gossiping of mankind at the very moment she is satirically sketching a conceited chattering parson and his engagement to a pretentious young woman:

> when Mr. Elton arrived to triumph in his happy prospects, and circulate the fame of her merits, there was very little more for him to do than to tell her Christian name, and say whose music she principally played.—(*Emma*, Chapter 22)

Not to multiply instances of these "delicate touches," I shall limit myself to two more. The first is just eight words of comment on a harmless country knight, which give us the man's failings in a flash:

Sir William Lucas had been formerly in trade in Meryton, where he had made a tolerable fortune, and risen to the honour of knighthood by an address to the King during his mayoralty. *The distinction had perhaps been felt too strongly* [my italics]. —(*Pride and Prejudice*, Chapter 5)

There is scarcely a chapter which lacks some quiet deadly comment on human nature. My last example is of a set of toadies hanging round a wealthy domineering woman:

The party then gathered round the fire to hear Lady Catherine determine what weather they were to have on the morrow.— (*Pride and Prejudice*, Chapter 29)

It is an additional merit that such perfect things were obviously not composed beforehand and pushed into the narrative, as often was the case, for instance, with Oscar Wilde's *bons mots*. They must have slipped naturally from her pen in the warmth and vivacity of creative writing, for naturalness is pre-eminently Jane Austen's virtue as a writer. She never strives for wit, she never abuses her gift of irony. If we could believe she had been allowed to read them, she would be among the most distinguished pupils of Voltaire and Gibbon as an ironist—strange reading for the girls in an English rectory during the French revolution, and yet no stranger than the fact that such a milieu produced such an ironist.

8

Roy Campbell

As I sit down to write this brief note seven months have passed since we received the bitter news that Roy Campbell was lost to us, accidentally killed on the roads of that Portugal he understood and loved so well. Since then the feeling of irreparable loss has increased rather than diminished, and it is hard to say whether the personal loss or the loss to Poetry is the greater, whether we should the more grieve that a man of such heroic proportions has ceased to live with us or that English Poetry has lost the one man of genius who had strength to maintain and to extend its ancient and arduous tradition. But, in fact, we cannot and should not separate the two aspects, for it is their union which made Roy Campbell so admirable a figure—that such a man of action should have been so splendid a poet!

In many epochs writers have lamented the decay or disappearance of "real poets," only to find that later generations did not share their pessimism and found much to admire in writers who had been dismissed as negligible by the critics. On the other hand there have been epochs—the first quarter of the nineteenth century was one—when poetry was more sought after by the public than prose. There was even a not very healthy "boom" of war poets in the 1914–18 period. But since then, and particularly in recent years, poets, critics, and public have agreed that poetry, if not absolutely unsaleable, is at any rate in very small demand. Outside the little specialist reviews, the little self-conscious "groups" and a little conventional notice from the press, contemporary po-

First published in French in *Hommage à Roy Campbell* (Editions de la Licorne; Montpellier, 1958).

etry is received with an immense drab indifference. Against
that background from time to time, like a flash of lightning,
sprang the name "Roy Campbell"—something amusing he
had said, something he had done, something he had written
had stirred the world amid the despairing yelps of disap-
proval of the "groups."

It so happens that Roy Campbell himself long ago made a
masterly analysis of a situation which resulted in the dis-
graceful paradox that he, the Poet, was received with catcalls
by the "groups." It is simply because of the "bureaucra-
tizing" of literature. On the one hand you have the journalist
in his office "carrying out a policy" and on another the
intellectual in his academic or official bureau writing "criticism" and sometimes even what is alleged to be poetry,
exactly as if this were a function of his drab office routine.
You get, says Campbell, a "poetry of bamboozlement,"
through which "hundreds of crossword-conscious professors"
can "joyfully hunt the thimble of meaning," a poetry "which
is vague and formless, but offers . . . a million suggestions of
half-meanings and glimmerings of sense." And what half-
meanings and glimpses of sense there were, came out of a
poverty-stricken experience of endless office hours varied by
the thrilling adventures of the corner pub, the secretariat,
and the Saturday evening cinema. . . .

I should not think of mentioning these petty anti-art
functionaries in a note on Roy Campbell if it were not for
the fact that French readers would not otherwise understand
how it happens that a man so interesting and a poet so gifted
is not far better known. Some years ago now I noticed in
quite a respectable French review an article on Roy Campbell. It had evidently been written in London solely for the
purpose of prejudicing French readers against the poet. The
article was a mixture of stupidity and malice written by "a
politico-critical pedant" as Campbell so rightly calls this type
of "critic," in the "meaningless technical jargon" which gives
such people the soothing feeling that they are still at work at
the government desk, seated on the government *rond de cuir*.
Gratuitous malevolence of this kind is so often reserved for
the man of genius. Utterly different as are Campbell and D.

H. Lawrence, they were both honored while they lived by exactly such spiteful denigration. Nor in either case did death put an end to this persecution from below, these squeaking libels of insectivorous jargon-spillers on their superior. Already some of the more insanitary misrepresentations of Roy Campbell dead recall the infamous obituaries of D. H. Lawrence. Well, the last thirty years have shown in Lawrence's case that hard as the battle may be, the man of genius slowly rises above the horde of detractors; and the next few years will show as great a triumph for Roy Campbell.

He was a man most authentically of his own age, but formed in an antique mould. Seldom has the world been privileged to enjoy so remarkable a combination of the Warrior and the Poet, of the man of intense action and the man of thought and sensibility. He was born of an ancient clan, with antecedents in Scotland and Northern Ireland, in a new land not subdued to the drab turmoil of cities and suburbs. He learned to ride and shoot when a boy, and in a land which had still kept immense quantities of wild animals. Campbell's drawings of South African animals are beautifully observed and rendered. He lived near an ocean swarming with fish and birds. In his memoirs he has described the light of dawn flashing on the myriads of birds of prey as they plunged on the vast shoals of migrating pilchards and soared up again to hover for another dive. It is the vision of a poet and of a hunter, set down in prose of a vigor and beauty such as few if any of his contemporaries could equal. And to think that this majestic lion of literature had to take the kicks of the jackasses and guttersnipes of London and New York! But of course their approval would have been a more sullying insult.

In those early South African years Campbell learned other things besides vigorous out-of-doors action and a passionate delight in wild living things and the beauty of the outer world. He found that he had the gift of comradeship and the gift of laughter. I have had wonderful friends and have felt devotion and have stood in the battle-line, but I have not known any man who aroused among his friends so wholehearted and so unquestioning a loyalty. Here was one Roy Campbell who could do no wrong! He must have been a magnificent N.C.O., and one can see why in spite of his long service he refused to accept the commission which unfortunately but inevitably cuts some of the comradeship between officer and men. Of course it is very hard to be a likeable Sergeant-Major, but Campbell seemingly achieved this almost impossible feat.

In Campbell this gift of comradeship was most happily allied with the gift of laughter. He could respond to what was lovable in his fellow men, but he could also see—and enjoy—what was laughable in them. To take one example only—who that has once heard it can forget his story of Musselcracker Finlayson and his two fishing mates on the Durban breakwater when they caught sight of the famous shark which had broken so many fishing lines streaming from its jaws that they looked like a ragged beard? Perhaps another writer might have got that far, but it needed Campbell with his satirical invention and his robust contempt for vegetarian and jaeger-underclothing socialism to stage a prolongation of the scene whereby the hairy shark was instantly identified by the trio as "Bernard Shaw."

Campbell is at his best, as poet, as prose-writer, and as a person, when he is in touch with the virility and vitality of the "outer" world—the world of South African hunters and natives, of the fishermen and *jouteurs* and *razeteurs* of Provence, of cattle-men and bull-fighters of Provence and Spain and Portugal, of seamen before the mast. When he is in England, among the Oxford or London intellectuals and artists, he loses strength and virtue, like Antaeus when severed from his mother Earth. With a few exceptions, these sedentary intellectuals, blinkered by their enormous superiority to all who were unlike them, could not respond to this poet-workman whose irony they mistook for naïveté. He fared and still fares even worse with self-appointed critics who inevitably disliked him because of their unspoken but unbreakable standard: Whatever is unlike us is evil. He came upon them early in life. Soon after he had been fetched back as under-age from the war of 1914–18 he shipped for

England, taking with him some volumes of the poets to study on the voyage. One of the ship's officers appointed himself ship's critic of literature, threw Campbell's poets into the sea, and gave him instead, as the be-all and end-all of literature, Wells's *Ann Veronica*!

We must add to this that in Spain he became a Roman Catholic convert, and defended with all his energy and ardor for his new faith the cause of General Franco. And then baffled and enraged his cockney critics by volunteering for the British Army to fight the Axis wherever it was to be fought overseas, while the critics fought on the radio or took up arms in the home counties: "Guarding the Vicar cycling round the shire."

The eternal and inexhaustible themes for the poet since the beginning of poetry have been Love, War, and God; and to these the English poets added Nature. But to write well on these great themes it is not only necessary to have the gift of words but to have experience. Even Shakespeare is more at home in a tavern than on a battle-field; and what fatuous "war poetry" has come from bards who never fired a shot to kill, what travesties in doggerel of false religious emotion, what affected amorous conceits from swains who never loved anyone but themselves, and what flirtations with Nature from rompers on Hampstead Heath! Of course the imagination has its rights, and poetry is the expression of imagination; but even more it is the expression of genuine emotion, and how can that exist without real experience? In Roy Campbell was a poet who at first hand had experienced War, Love, and Religion, and the wild living things of Nature, which to the pavement artists and critics appeared not only unfair but untrue. He was "contrary," they complained. Of course he was—contrary as any genuine article is to the innumerable pinchbeck shams.

There still remains another aspect of Campbell's poetic genius—or rather, two aspects—which must be recorded. He is a great verse satirist, a difficult and splendid art in which John Dryden was his master and almost his only rival. There was a satirist in Campbell in early days, but he discovered his full strength and eloquence under the stress of his wars and of his return to an England rotten with craven socialism, and lending itself to nothing but derisive laughter with its fatuous illusions of grandeur and pathetic aping of past grandeur. Yet while denouncing with infinite scorn the hordes of impostors Campbell never for an instant hesitated in his loyalty to the Throne and what he believed the Throne stands for. After all, South Africa and not England was his country, but the Monarchy had no more loyal subject or devoted soldier. It is in the collection called *Talking Bronco*—a would-be contemptuous epithet of his enemies flung back at them with thousandfold contempt—that this superb satire is most fully and gloriously represented. Like all great satire it is at once personal and general, fights for a cause while crushing the horde of gadflies which clusters round every great poet. Why should we be surprised that Campbell has immortalized these insignificant vermin? It was only what Dryden and Pope and Byron had done before him, and, as Yeats said, "Where's the wild dog that has praised its fleas?" In these *Talking Bronco* poems Campbell shows a mastery of English verse equal to Dryden himself, while he has taken the racy language of the soldier and the colonial and stamped it with a strength and fitness which makes it classic.

> Like shells with which the beach is starry,
> Chalking their whiteness down the shore,
> I watch the motionless safari
> Of transport that will trek no more,
> The caravan of bones that reaches
> To fetch the moon through craggy breaches
> Along the avenue of dunes,
> With sorrow for the white askari
> And hunger for his black platoons.
> The ether hums with strange reports,
> The winds are dithering wild with news:
> Through Africa, huge reefs of quartz
> Grind like the gilded teeth of Jews;
> The East is conquering the West;
> The future has a face to flee;
> The vultures on the cookhouse nest
> Like Poets in the B.B.C.

And side by side with this burning originality, this majestic *saeva indignato*, and the Rabelaisian laughter of his memoirs, Campbell produced scholarly translations which included St. John of the Cross, Baudelaire, and Horace.

Here is the merest glimpse of the poet we mourn, the hero we worshipped, the man we loved. I think I see him now seated at table, like one of the heroes of Homer, his own bottle of *gros rouge* (which he preferred to finer wines) at his elbow, keeping us in a constant ripple of laughter, and including us all in the warmth of his love and comradeship.

9

Lawrence Durrell

Although his present international reputation is recent, Lawrence Durrell is by no means a newcomer, not one of those "popular" authors, who suddenly achieve notoriety and, likely enough, as suddenly lose it — "up like a rocket and down like a stick," as they say. For a considerable time Durrell has been quietly but steadily widening the public for his delicate and brilliant poetry, consolidating this success, and increasing the number of his readers, by such prose books as *Prospero's Cell* and *Reflections on a Marine Venus*.

To meet the exigencies of "the trade" (i.e., the book-sellers) these two books and the more recent *Bitter Lemons* are described as "travel." Well, of course, in a sense they are travel books, but long experience of the British "travel book" makes one wary. Too often such books are superficial, based on notes taken on a tourist trip, and padded with information mugged up in a public library — "high-pressure cookery at the airport" as someone recently called this type of book. Now, Durrell's "travel" books are the antithesis of the Brummagem articles. They are first-hand and authentic throughout, and it would be far more accurate to describe them as "foreign-residence" books, especially as each is limited to a Mediterranean island, Corfu, Rhodes, Cyprus. *Bitter Lemons* (the book on Cyprus) is not only a vivid evocation of the island, its beauty and its people, but contains a well-informed account of the Eoka rebellion, for Durrell was in the Cyprus government service at the time.

Bitter Lemons brought Durrell one of those literary prizes which too often are consolation prizes for missing the sales'

First published in the review *Two Cities*, Paris, 1959.

bus. Not so in this case. The award coincided with the wide and still rapidly expanding success of the first three novels—*Justine, Balthazar, Mountolive*—of the quartet which has yet to be completed by "Clea"; all staged in Alexandria.

Durrell is a writer of "the outer world," beyond the stale and swarming capitals of the West, with streets mere strident traffic-lanes and car-parks, and their populations sentenced to a mechanized monotony of "amusements" as uninteresting as the self-inflicted tortures of a masochistic friar or fakir. He is Irish, a dangerous inheritance, as his countrymen are sometimes born intriguers, adventurers, and tale-spinners; but he has kept these gifts to their proper sphere, his novels. He was born in India, and though that experience has left hundreds of thousands of stolid English children as wooden as it found them, this was clearly not the case with Durrell. As he hints somewhere, he was influenced as a child by the fact that he "looked out on the Himalaya," and not, shall we add, on the "tame and domestic" beauties of suburbanized England. The Levant is as familiar to him as the England in which he was educated. He has lived and worked in Rhodes, Alexandria, and Cairo.

If the success of the *Justine* novels had been limited to England one might be tempted to attribute it to the British romantic sentimentality about the Middle East and their nostalgic harping on the empire they lost there. But the novels are as popular in America and in Germany as in England, so it is quite clear that their success with such different types of readers must be due to more solid merits. And of course that is the fact. There are not many occasions in life when on reading a new novel one becomes more and more enthusiastic, feeling "here is a new personality in writing, something pungent and original which will almost certainly endure." I experienced that going on for half a century ago with D. H. Lawrence's *Sons and Lovers*, James Joyce's *Ulysses*, and Proust's *Du Côté de chez Swann*. And now again, after a barren period, with *Justine, Balthazar,* and *Mountolive*. My one complaint against this author is that he has not already provided me with his fourth volume, "Clea," which I am impatient to read—and in any case how can one do justice to a quartet of novels, the fourth of which is apparently to bind all together, when only three are available?

I am not sure that I am greatly attracted or convinced by the Note at the beginning of *Balthazar,* where Durrell invokes modern philosophy or science and likens his quartet to what he calls "the relativity proposition." I realize, of course, that such analogies are useful to the artist as imaginary (and, in my humble opinion, insecure) scaffolding for his building, while—to mix the metaphor gleefully—they provide a plate of bones for "the critics" to mumble; but in fact all he needed to say is said on page 155 of *Justine*:

What I most need to do is to record experiences, not in the order in which they took place—for that is history—but in the order in which they first became significant for me.

Even this seems rather sophisticated for an artist. What really happened was that the Word of the Lord came unto him, saying: "Lawrence Durrell?" and he bowed himself and replied: "Lord, here am I." And the Lord said: "Lawrence, enter into thy closet and shut the door, and write a masterpiece in four volumes." And, having mingled with Arabs and suchlike, he replied: "To hear is to obey." Curious how great artists always or nearly always want to go slumming with philosophers and scientists. But what can one expect? It is rumored—but Allah is All-knowing—that great artists have even associated with virtuous women.

Be that as it may, the theme of these novels is Alexandria (Egypt), and according to the moralists, Alexandria is "a sink of iniquity." Durrell does not altogether discourage this view. A minor British diplomat, whose memoirs I chance to be rereading, says that he enjoyed the confidence of Hussein Kamel, the first Sultan of post-occupation Egypt. "Mon ami," the Sultan would say, "j'ai roulé ma bosse un peu partout, mais jamais je n'ai rencontré un méli-mélo pareil." That, of course, was years before the Justine epoch but evidently there is a close link between Cairo and Alexandria, and Egypt remains the same however much it changes.

Adultery, prostitution, sodomy, lesbianism, sadism, murder, suicide, and all that sort of thing, are not absent from these pages. But "how about Europe?" Any evening paper will supply it all, including the incest at which Durrell hints discreetly. In addition, we have such newsworthy items as the mysterious disappearance of Justine's child, the Coptic-Jewish conspiracy for gunrunning to (at that time) British Palestine, and the proverbially incompetent British secret service—always discovering the enemy's secrets when they have ceased to matter. The scene is observed with masterly coolness and precision.

However, this *méli-mélo* is not what attracts me. I rather dislike it in fact. I do not need cayenne pepper and chili sauce on *coq au vin*. But, of course, the *méli-mélo* and the eroticism are as much a part of the Alexandrian scene as a pea-souper fog and Sunday boredom are a part of London. It would be absurd to present Alexandria as having the physical climate of London, or the moral rectitude of New York where business alone needs a mere thirty thousand call-girls. Honor where honor is due.

Possibly, the *méli-mélo* is what has attracted some readers, but I can assure you that by itself it would not have attracted me. Scores of books with that and nothing more have passed from my table to the wastepaper basket. Durrell is of another world, a poet as much entitled to use these potent spices or vitriols as Shakespeare himself. In Durrell I praise his humanity first of all—he suffers, and we suffer with him, for the wounds life deals his characters, especially the women. And tenderness for women and their undeserved sufferings is the mark of a good man. Melissa! She is an unassuaged wound in my heart, as she must be in Durrell's. She is so real that though she is but a character in a novel and dead, one wants to do something about her. That wretched little dressing room of hers, filled with the pipes from the lavatories above, where she had only a "poignant slip of cracked glass" as a mirror! We talk of or rather quote the *lacrimae rerum*, but here is a word-magician who can pierce our hearts with such anguish as that "poignant" slip of mirror. Forty years ago they said of Duhamel that he had "changé le pathétique," but Durrell has made it almost unbearable in that phrase.

And then turned the screw by making the doctor say of Melissa dying "If she could be loved a little." What is the good of our loving Melissa dying, Melissa dead, except that we are butchered to make a Durrell holiday?

I am trying to indicate in a few words, in stuttering shorthand, how these novels take hold of one, how they become part of one's life. "I am the man, I suffered, I was there," says Walt Whitman somewhere in *Leaves of Grass*. But with Durrell the sense of being one with his experience and his characters is strangely vivid—I should perhaps have said "ineluctable" or "indubitable." Only a great writer who has lived and enjoyed life can convey this feeling of tragedy. Perhaps it was with ironic intent that Durrell puts his tragedy under the patronage of the Marquis de Sade and Freud, the patient and the thaumaturge—Bluebeard and Santa Claus.

One or two persons who claim to have spent at least a weekend in Alexandria assure me that the city he has evoked is imaginary, not the reality. If so, the more poet he! What is indisputable is that once Durrell has caught a reader in his spell, escape is almost impossible. One is forced to follow him line by line, and page by page, as he opens out vista after vista of his enchanted and squalid city, reveals his characters, and surprises, pleases, or shocks us with their adventures.

The author may repudiate this, but as I reread these books I see them less and less as separate works, and more as one continually expanding and rewarding narrative, where some fresh piece of information or someone else's more intimate knowledge of a character suddenly changes the significance of what we have already learned. In the early part the author is mainly occupied with "creating" the city and its ambiance for us, and in blocking out his characters with their complex and promiscuous sex relations to each other. Melissa, the pathetically frail Greek dancer from Smyrna, lives with Darley, but at one time or another she seems to have been the mistress of most of the men in the book—eventually has a child by Nessim, a little girl looked after by Darley after Melissa's death. How poor and how naïve Melissa is, comes out quite indirectly and almost, as it were, by chance. She speaks somewhere of Justine's "immense fortune," and it is much later that we learn casually that this immense fortune was in fact three thousand pounds given to Justine by Nessim before their marriage. Such a lonely little life for all her sexual intimacies. And yet it is the guileless Melissa who accidentally reveals the existence of an anti-British political conspiracy which breaks up friendships and causes the suicide of the writer-diplomat, Pursewarden. The very center of the conspiracy is Nessim!

As we move deeper into the narrative Durrell's irony brings more surprises. Darley, neglecting Melissa, has more or less fallen in love with Nessim's Jewess wife, Justine, and believes she is in love with him. Later we learn through the homosexual doctor, Balthazar, that though Justine was Darley's mistress she was really in love with Pursewarden, who cares nothing for her! Further irony—Sir David Mountolive, British ambassador to Egypt, in his young days had been the lover of Leila, the once-beautiful mother of Nessim and Narouz.

I oversimplify, and turn subtleties into commonplaces, but one has to give some rudimentary outline of these complex relationships to indicate the skill with which Durrell has created, woven and unwoven them. Simple characters and straightforward situations are obviously far more easily handled by the novelist than the more complicated, and only a really great writer could so successfully maintain characters so curious and relationships so tortuous. Behind all this erotic musical chairs, sinister treachery and violence lurk. There is the Nessim gunrunning to Palestine plot, Pursewarden's suicide, the murder of old Scobie, the murder of Toto de Brunel by Narouz (a mistake, he thought he was murdering his sister-in-law, Justine) and then the assassination of Narouz himself.

At the point the narrative has now reached with the end of *Mountolive* this seems a superlative irony. Of course the real conspirator (and, to his British friends, traitor) was Nessim. Narouz, the simpler character, though in some way almost a Victor Hugo figure of horror, merely followed his brother. When Pursewarden through Melissa discovers the plot he of course sees that his chief, Mountolive, is informed; but arranges that the first person to find his dead body is Nessim, for whom he has left a message of warning written in shaving soap on the mirror. Both sides then know. In duty bound, Mountolive makes one official protest after another to the Minister, Memlik Pasha, which in that latitude can mean only assassination. But Nessim knows a trick to defeat the British. Memlik Pasha collects old and beautiful editions of the Koran, particularly those brought by suppliants who have taken care to interleave the holy book with banknotes. Whenever the situation becomes menacing Nessim presents another Koran, until driven into an impossible dilemma between Mountolive's official representations and Nessim's Korans, the Pasha orders the murder of Narouz. And the third volume ends with a superb description of the Coptic women ceremonially wailing the dead man. Justine, we learn, has abandoned her home and husband to work on a Jewish farm in Palestine.

Thus far we have reached. For what more is to come we must wait for the publication of "Clea." Any reader of this article who has not read the Durrell novels must be warned that I have given only part of the complex action and have mentioned only some of the characters. Moreover, crudely summarizing I have probably made the books sound much more sensational and "spy-ring" than in fact they are. Of course there is unquestionably sensational material here, and wrongly treated it might have lapsed into deplorable melodrama. From this mishap the narrative is saved not only by the distinction of the style but by the even more marked distinction of the author's mind. His interest is not in presenting these exotic or extravagant or violent situations for their own merely sensational sake, but in discovering how and why they came about, the "secret places of the soul" in which the ironies and tragedies were conceived.

> In art you can do anything you like—
> The thing is, to be sure you like it.

There is one character I have barely mentioned, but must just notice, and that is Scobie, the old Englishman who after years of service in the Egyptian police is suddenly promoted to command their secret police. Here Durrell's method changes, and Scobie is presented purely as a figure of fun, the predestined victim of the poet's satirical verve and gift of laughter. I have seldom read anything more amusing as comedy-farce than the fifteen pages of *Balthazar*, describing a visit with Scobie to his rooms. There is the green parrot, brought from Yokohama by his sailor friend, Toby, which surprisingly can speak Arabic, and what is more a most sacred text of the Koran, interspersed with rude noises. Fortunately Scobie's police uniform protected Toby from mass circumcision by a horde of angry zealots. His shabby and smelly rooms in the native quarter shelter his illicit attempts to brew what he calls Plaza beer and a shudderingly awful Mock Whiskey. These revelations lead to others. Scobie has received a confidential official document, ordering him to be most careful not to employ "peddyrasts" in his police work. His conscience is troubled—should he not confess that he himself "has Tendencies"? To top it all Scobie then confesses that he sometimes dresses and goes out in women's clothes—"when the Fleet's in, old man"—and asks Darley to remove temptation by taking away the dress. Alas, poor Scobie. He succumbed to temptation again and was found dead in the street in female costume, kicked to death by infuriated sailors of H.M.S. *Milton*—a nice touch of irony in the ship's name, for while the French give battleships the names of great authors (Voltaire, Renan) the English would think it a derogation and an insult to the Fleet.

In a rather less irreverent manner, Durrell has produced in this style two collections of short sketches dealing with humorous or farcical situations and persons in the Diplomatic Corps—a rather risky thing to do, perhaps, but he does it with such good humor and provokes such irresistible laughter in readers who take his allusions that there is absolutely no offense. I sent a copy of *Esprit de Corps* to an old friend, a Senior Diplomat who had just returned worn out and dispirited from a particularly arduous and frustrating mission. His gratitude was delightful—it had taken his mind off official worries as nothing else could, and he had been so much amused he had sat up until late at night reading the book, and laughing aloud. This is the kind of genuine tribute authors long for, but very seldom receive.

And now we must wait for "Clea."

10

D. H. Lawrence

We live in an epoch when "the public" receives its information and opinions from newspapers, and similar trash, on the air, by TV, etc. Thus, D. H. Lawrence is mainly known as the author of *Lady Chatterley's Lover,* not because this is the finest and most beautiful of his books, but because it has been "news." It became "news" because the police and bureaucrats of the Yanko-sachsen countries chose to prosecute it as obscene. The obscenity was in them, not in the book. That did not matter—the "story" made "news," and so D. H. Lawrence is for most people the author of an indecent work called *Lady Chatterley's Lover.*

Of course, *Lady Chatterley's Lover* is a fine novel, though not the best Lawrence wrote, but it is unfortunate that he should be known mainly as the author of one book, when his output was so considerable and so varied, not only as novelist and short-story writer, but as poet, essayist, psychologist, writer of travel books, and literary critic. What should we think if the public at large were led to believe that Balzac was the author solely of *La Fille aux Yeux d'Or* simply because at the time of publication some scandal attached to it?

It would be absurd to blame the public for this state of affairs, since naturally they have neither the time, inclination, nor equipment to make a thorough investigation of authors, especially when they are foreigners. For that they rely on the professional critics, but until this book by F.-J. Temple, Lawrence has been unfortunate in his French interpreters who seem to be unfamiliar with the facts of his life as

First published in French as an introduction to F.-J. Temple's *D. H. Lawrence* (Editions Seghers; Paris, 1960).

well as many of his books. I don't mean to engage in the ungracious and unnecessary task of pointing out the errors of Temple's predecessors in France. Perhaps one example will stand for all. I remember reading an interpretation of Lawrence based entirely on the assumption that he was *"un primaire."* If that means anything, it means a person who has received only an elementary education. The truth is that Lawrence won a scholarship at Nottingham High School, one of the oldest and best secondary schools in England, and remained there for four years. Later he was first in all England in winning the King's scholarship, took a Teacher's Certificate at Nottingham University, and became a schoolmaster! Other studies of Lawrence are equally superficial, based very likely on the casual talk of some ill-informed or hostile English "critic."

With this book of F.-J. Temple we at once reach a far higher level. The book is scholarly, not in the sense that it is academic or pretentiously methodical, but because the writer has gone to the best and most authentic sources, has studied them carefully and intelligently, with an excellent critical sense, and has presented them in a readable form. What more can we ask of a biographer? Certainly, the book is the product of an unselfish devotion to its subject, for much time and study were needed for Temple to make himself so thoroughly acquainted with all the various aspects of Lawrence's life and writings. The greatest English writer of this century is at last adequately presented to the French literary public.

Temple shows how well he has comprehended Lawrence by making this study mainly biographical, though the book contains interesting though unpretentious critical judgments, with some very well chosen extracts from his varied writings. There is a school of criticism, rather a lazy one, which ignores the lives of writers entirely and claims to interpret their writings without any reference to them personally — rather like the "historians" who cannot be bothered with the trivialities of sequence and dates. No doubt in some cases the "life" may be ignored without great loss, but it simply is not so in the case of D. H. Lawrence whose writings when arranged in chronological sequence form a great mental, moral, and physical autobiography, while Lawrence himself was a very remarkable person. I do not think that so many personal narratives and reminiscences have been published of any other English author since Lord Byron. It is a curious coincidence that Lord Byron's seat, Newstead Abbey, is in Nottinghamshire, only a few miles from Eastwood where the plebeian Lawrence was born and grew up. Still more curious is the fact that Lawrence's first love, Jessie Chambers, lived in a small farm on the estate of Annesley where Byron as a very young man fell in love with Mary Chaworth.

These coincidences are purely accidental and without significance, but they may serve to stress the fact that D. H. Lawrence is the one fiercely passionate and gifted English genius since Byron—though the one was descended from an ancient family of the Anglo-Norman *noblesse*, and the other was the son of a coalminer. Owing to some blunder of the police during the First World War, Lawrence was absurdly suspected of espionage, though I myself can testify from personal knowledge that his ignorance of military and cognate affairs was so wilfully complete that he would not have known what to spy upon. The charge aroused his utmost indignation and anger, and in repelling it he spoke of himself as "One of the most intensely English little men England ever produced, with a passion for his country, even if it were often a passion of hatred."

The French reader must beware of supposing that by "English" is here meant the conventional and highly erroneous French idea of what constitutes an Englishman—a comic-paper character who wears a bowler hat, smokes a pipe, always carries an umbrella, drinks pale ale, plays ridiculous games like cricket, is prudish, hypocritical, phlegmatic, and suffers from a wholly French invention called "le spleen," while he has the most rudimentary ideas of gastronomy, art, literature, and love making. He was no more that sort of "English" than Lord Byron was, and by "English" Lawrence meant an intransigent individualism, that "truth to oneself" which has caused England to abound in heretics, of a much less interesting type than Lawrence.

Recently (since 1957) there has been published at intervals in the United States a "composite biography" of Lawrence in three large volumes, with a total of about 1,500 pages of text, edited by Edward Nehls. This is made up partly of extracts from Lawrence's vivid Letters (of which a new and greatly enlarged edition is to be published) but mainly of personal recollections and testimonies from persons who knew him. From this immense work one realizes, first, that almost every person who came into contact with Lawrence was impressed by his personality in one way or another and remembered him, and, second, how varied are the impressions recorded, ranging from hero-worship through every grade of feeling down to extreme hostility and hatred. To this one must add that from his youth onwards those who received his letters preserved them, either from affection for him, or from a conviction that he would one day be recognized as "great," or, in at least one illustrious case, as vindictive evidence against him. Few if any of these testimonies are the conventional "de mortuis nil nisi bonum" notices which are so often published, but genuine and uninhibited expressions of the feelings he aroused. Instead of being a tiresome collection of insincerities, such as the book about *"Colonel" T. E. Lawrence by his "Friends,"* this book is alive and fascinating. This sincerity of utterance is exactly what D. H. Lawrence himself practiced and inculcated in others, though he was not pleased when others spoke their minds about him as freely as he spoke his about them.

Every human being makes friends and enemies and intermediate relations, but the extreme diversity and frequently emphatic expression of these opinions about D. H. Lawrence are an indication of his extraordinarily complex and even contradictory character. He could be, and often was within a very short interval, the most charming and stimulating of companions and the most offensive and insulting of gratuitous censors. I have said of him that at his best he made one feel as if living in a world where the air had become oxygen and he shared with one a vividness of life and beauty beyond words; while at his worst he could be and was intensely disagreeable and unpleasant. With that magnificent sincerity

which is characteristic of him Lawrence has faithfully recorded the two antithetical sides of his personality in the
portraits of himself which figure in his novels—Cyril Beard-
sall in *The White Peacock*, Paul Morel in *Sons and Lovers*,
Birkin in *Women in Love*, Lilley in *Aaron's Rod*, Somers in
Kangaroo, Mellors in *Lady Chatterley's Lover*. He wrote of
himself as an adolescent as follows:

When there was any clog in his soul's quick running, his face
went stupid and ugly. He was the sort of boy that becomes a
clown and a lout as soon as he is not understood or feels himself
held cheap; and, again, is adorable at the first touch of warmth.

Again, writing of himself as Birkin in *Women in Love* he
says:

And it was this duality of feeling which he created in her,
that made a fine hate of him quicken in her bowels. There was
his wonderful, desirable life-rapidity, the rare quality of an utterly
desirable man; and there was at the same time this ridiculous,
mean effacement into a Salvator Mundi and a Sunday school
teacher, a prig of the stiffest type.

And yet again of himself in Australia under the very thin
disguise of Somers:

Him, a lord and master! Why, he was not really lord of his
own bread and butter; next year they might both be starving.
And he was not even master of himself, with his ungovernable
furies and his uncritical intimacies with people . . . He was so
isolated he was hardly a man at all, among men. He had
absolutely nothing but her. Among men he was like some un-
believable creature—an emu, for example. Like an emu in the
streets or in a railway carriage.

Don't miss the intentional humor of his likening himself
to "an emu in a railway carriage"—he could laugh at himself
as well as most accurately expose and denounce his failings.
Of which among his critics can this be said? Having known
Lawrence and his books since 1914, and having as it were
lived my little part in the Lawrence saga, I know full well
that the bitterest and most venomous attacks on him are
simply the result of wounded vanity—resentment against his
caricatures when the victims were unable to retaliate. It was

unfortunate in a way that Lawrence could not help caricaturing persons who had tried to help him and give him money, but this is not unusual in artists. French readers will remember the occasion when Rimbaud took leave of one of his benefactors in Paris by defecating in the morning milk. Lawrence never went that far, to my knowledge, but he certainly figuratively spat in the faces of his benefactors. In some cases the resultant rage and resentment were excessive. The way to treat those satirical portraits was to laugh at them and to caricature *him*—his amazement and moral concern when that happened were very comical. I know, because that was my case, and I certainly never bore him any ill will in consequence, and he certainly forgave me.

All this would be rather beside the point if we were not dealing with a very great artist. Use of the word "artist" may cause French readers to think I mean such superb craftsmen in literature as Racine, Flaubert, or Mallarmé. In Lawrence's case "artist" does not mean that at all, for he disdained all such delicate and beautiful conscious workmanship. I mean that he was greatly gifted, and squandered his gift recklessly, as we see in other English geniuses such as Blake and Byron and Dickens, and even Shakespeare. Lawrence's perceptions (his "awareness" as he called it) both of people and of the living world of birds, flowers, beasts, were intensely vivid and acute. He saw and felt more keenly and aesthetically than any English writer of this century, and he had a natural gift of writing which raised intense hatred in his philistine country and is now one of its few remaining glories. Though he had tricks of repetition and over-emphasis, his mastery of the infinite resources of the varied English language is unsurpassed in our time. He could handle it superbly, from slang and *patois* to a quite majestic eloquence beyond any English writer of his time. Throughout his narratives the tone is always unforced, natural, personal, so that even now thirty years after his death I can still hear his living voice when I reread his books. He was, in parenthesis, at times a most brilliant talker, not making *bons mots* or pretty compliments to the ladies, but speaking of life and his experiences with a vivid natural eloquence as marvelous as the best of his writing. I have recorded one such experience somewhere, of an evening at his Villa Mirenda near Florence, when he began talking of his life with Frieda in Mexico and New Mexico, soaring up and up like an eagle, and holding us all spellbound in silence until suddenly we realized we were sitting in complete darkness, held by a voice.

You must not go to Lawrence for ideas and intellectual remarks and "philosophy." He had a "philosophy" of course, a good deal too much of it, and the pedants can amuse themselves for the next generation in making it mean what they want it to mean. What Lawrence has to give is not ideas (of which he had, I repeat, too many), but the living world. You must live his books, you must respond to the vividness with which he gives you the life and beauty of the world. Almost invariably he hit on the exact phrase. I may perhaps mention one which greatly amused me and which is very striking in its picturesque accuracy. Somewhere in his Mexican novel, *The Plumed Serpent*, he speaks of mangoes as looking like bull's testicles. I laughed when I first read it, thinking: "Dear Lorenzo, he must always be making sexual symbols of innocent fruits." Years after his death I went for the first time to the tropics, and was shown a mango tree with fruits on it—and, by the living God, bull's testicles are exactly what they do look like! Who else had ever noticed the fact or had the wit to say so?

Believe me, for those who can respond to him, Lawrence is an essential experience. He was a real person, a genuine artist, never a best-selling author signing his new book for the snob public and smirking at the camera of the publicity man. His integrity was absolute. Since his death injudicious friends have published manuscripts which had better have been left unprinted. But in the main the amazing fact is that in a mere twenty years a man could write so much so well.

I must not detain you any longer from what Temple has to tell you. Writing as one of the few survivors of the now rapidly shrinking band of those who knew and defended Lawrence in his lifetime, I should like to end by saying that Temple has done a remarkably good piece of interpretive writing which at last worthily presents Lawrence to France.

Let us hope that this may lead to the reissue of the quite numerous translations of Lawrence in French which have appeared from time to time, and that the translations may now be carefully revised by somebody who knows English— and French.